SELECTED WRITINGS

WILLIAM TYNDALE was born in about 1494 near Slimbridge, Gloucestershire, and educated at Oxford. During the early 1520s he began his English translation of the New Testament, which he completed in Cologne and Worms in 1526. He followed this with a translation of the Old Testament, the first five books of which were printed in Antwerp in 1530. Among his other works were *The Parable of the Wicked Mammon* (1528), *The Obedience of a Christian Man* (1528), *A Pathway to the Holy Scripture* (1530), *The Practice of Prelates* (1531) and *An Exposition upon the First Epistle of John* (1531). In 1535 he was arrested, charged with heresy and condemned to death; he was executed on 6 October 1536.

DAVID DANIELL is Emeritus Professor of English at University College London and Honorary Fellow of Hertford and St Catherine's Colleges, Oxford. He is the author of many articles and books on Shakespeare, including the Arden edition of *Julius Caesar*. For Penguin Classics he edited Tyndale's *Obedience of a Christian Man*. Yale University Press published his editions of *Tyndale's New Testament* and *Tyndale's Old Testament*, his *William Tyndale: A Biography*, and *The Bible in English: Its History and Influence*. He is Chairman of the Tyndale Society.

FyfieldBooks aim to make available some of the great classics of British and European literature in clear, affordable formats, and to restore often neglected writers to their place in literary tradition.

FyfieldBooks take their name from the Fyfield elm in Matthew Arnold's 'Scholar Gypsy' and 'Thyrsis'. The tree stood not far from the village where the series was originally devised in 1971.

Roam on! The light we sought is shining still.
Dost thou ask proof? Our tree yet crowns the hill,
Our Scholar travels yet the loved hill-side

from 'Thyrsis'

WILLIAM TYNDALE

Selected Writings

Edited with an introduction by
DAVID DANIELL

Fyfield*Books*

CARCANET

Acknowledgements

Extracts from *Tyndale's New Testament* (ed. David Daniell; New Haven and London: Yale University Press, 1995) and *Tyndale's Old Testament* (ed. David Daniell; New Haven and London: Yale University Press, 1992) reproduced by permission of Yale University Press. Extracts from *The Obedience of a Christian Man* (ed. David Daniell; Harmondsworth: Penguin, 2000) reproduced by permission of Penguin Press.

First published in Great Britain in 2003 by
Carcanet Press Limited
Alliance House
Cross Street
Manchester M2 7AQ

Introduction and editorial matter © David Daniell 2003

The right of David Daniell to be identified as the editor of this work
has been asserted by him in accordance with the
Copyright, Designs and Patents Act of 1988
All rights reserved

A CIP catalogue record for this book is available from the British Library
ISBN 1 85754 656 3

The publisher acknowledges financial assistance from Arts Council England

Typeset by XL Publishing Services, Tiverton
Printed and bound in England by SRP Ltd, Exeter

Contents

Introduction

At the beginning of the twenty-first century, William Tyndale (*c.* 1494–1536) has several different reputations.

For lovers of the Bible, and for historians of the Bible translated into the vernaculars, he is being rediscovered as the founding father of the English Bible. He was a scholar of Greek and Hebrew at a time when such learning was unusual. He translated the New Testament, and much of the Old Testament, from their original languages of Greek and Hebrew into English for the first time. He printed them for everyone to read. He opened a door which has never again been shut up. Since his first complete English New Testament (1526), the Bible has been available to everyone in the world who can read or hear English. For this, with his work unfinished, he was condemned by the church as a heretic, and handed over to the civil authorities to be killed. His translations went on to be the basis of all English versions that followed. The New Testament of the 'King James' version of 1611 (the 'Authorised Version') is eighty-three per cent Tyndale. The most modern translations still show strong marks of his craft.

Secondly, for lovers of the English language, Tyndale is the genius who, in those widely read Bible translations, gave England in the middle of the sixteenth century its first disseminated Plain Style, so that anyone who had anything to say had a simple model to follow. Later in the century, no longer did a man or woman need to be part of a refined élite, learned in the ancient classics and the literature of France and, particularly, Italy, in order to write well and be read. Decades before, at the start of that sixteenth century, while Tyndale was at Oxford, the English language had become a mess, quite lacking direction, muddling older Saxon and Norman French, with Latinist vocabulary and rambling syntax. In about 1505, John Skelton, a poet at the court of King Henry VIII, wrote verses to say so, beginning 'Our naturall tong is rude'.

Tyndale changed this. From the mid-1520s he wrote English in a register just above common speech, in short Saxon sentences with largely Saxon vocabulary, a manner like proverbs. The result was easily memorised, as the New Testament Gospels, for example, were intended to be. 'Ask, and it shall be given you: seek, and ye shall find: knock, and it shall be opened unto you.' 'For this my son was dead, and is alive again.' Very many phrases of his are still in everyday use, such as 'Let there be light', or 'The spirit is willing'.

Thirdly, for conservative modern historians, Tyndale, if he is mentioned at all, is the objectionable little man (he is known in some Catholic circles as 'tiny Tyndale') who, a mere heretic, annoyed the great Saint Thomas More. They refer only to Tyndale's 'polemic' works, like his *The Practice of Prelates* (1530), or *Answer to More* (1531). Such historians may, though not always, add a footnote to mention that Tyndale translated the Bible, with the suggestion that it was an inconsiderable and rather odd thing to have done. What matter to them are his 'unbridled' attacks on Mother Church. He is 'lewd', even foul-mouthed. When, on opening his text, examples of those characteristics are slow to appear, they are put by his enemies into his mouth.

Patience is needed to explain that all Tyndale's non-biblical writing had a far wider canvas than the supposed scoring of nasty points, being no less than New Testament theology. And that More, by 1529 a seasoned abuser of Luther in Latin, had been invited by the Bishop of London to attack Tyndale in print, and in English, in which Tyndale always wrote. Bishop Tunstall gave More dispensation to read 'the heretic' Tyndale. More attacked Tyndale – clearly to Tyndale's surprise – forcefully, over some years, sometimes obscenely, and at very great (and unfinished) length. Sir Thomas does not come out well from a study of his attacks on reformers. Though Tyndale is a large part of More's story, More is a small part of Tyndale's: his *Answer to More* is factual and brief. Tyndale's large Bible work – he translated the New Testament twice, and half the Old Testament – has survived beyond anything dreamed of for More's writing. Tyndale, through English Bibles, has reached an even greater number of English readers than Shakespeare. (It is Thomas More, however, who remains lodged in the popular mind.)

A fourth reputation is just beginning. Tyndale was more than a mildly theological thinker. He is at last being understood as, theologically as well as linguistically, well ahead of his time. For him, as several decades later for Calvin (and in the twentieth century for Karl Barth) the overriding message of the New Testament is the sovereignty of God. Everything is contained in that. It must never, as he wrote, be lost from sight. Tyndale is far from being, as he has usually until now been described, quite derivative, serving up slivers of Luther with a drizzle of Zwingli. Tyndale, we are now being shown, was original and new – except that he was also old, demonstrating the understanding of God as revealed in the whole New Testament. For Tyndale, God is, above all, sovereign, active in the individual and in history. He is the one, as he put it, in whom alone is found salvation and flourishing. When he wrote, this was very far from being said, even by Luther. What was sovereign in the 1530s, as it had been for about twelve hundred years, was the church, and ultimately the pope: Tyndale showed how much that was a distortion of the New Testament.

TYNDALE'S LIFE

A well-born Gloucestershire boy, Tyndale learned the new, good humanist Latin at Oxford, In his ten years there, he also learned Greek, which was also new and much less common. Describing his Oxford experience, he told of his distress that theology, which occupied his final years there, had nothing to do with the Bible at all, being entirely disputatious Scholasticism based on Aristotle. In 1516, however, while he was still at Magdalen Hall, Erasmus's *Novum Instrumentum* was printed in Basle. Tyndale clearly owned a copy. This book, intended as a 'New Instrument' towards church reform from the inside, contained Erasmus's fresh Latin translation of the New Testament from the Greek, to correct the Latin 'Vulgate' which the church had used for a thousand years. The new textual scholarship was showing the Vulgate to be full of errors. Erasmus's new Latin was a bold (and scandalous) move. Even bolder (and not mentioned on his lengthy title page) was his printing of the original Greek alongside his new Latin. This was the first time that the Greek New Testament had been printed. It is no exaggeration to say that it set fire to Europe. Luther translated it into his famous German version of 1522. In a few years, there appeared translations from that Greek into most European vernaculars. They were the true basis of the popular reformation.

In the early 1520s, and by now ordained priest, Tyndale set out, using Erasmus's Greek, to make an English translation of the New Testament, the first ever from the original. He also intended his English New Testament to be printed, again the first ever. (The influential translations made in the 1380s, under the aegis of John Wyclif in Oxford, had been from the Latin Vulgate, and were necessarily, at that date, in manuscript.)

Refused permission to do the work in England, Tyndale went first to a good printer in Cologne. Betrayed there, he fled to the safe Lutheran city of Worms, and finished the work. From 1526 his pocket size English New Testaments, smuggled into ports in England and Scotland in bales of cloth, were eagerly received, and read, and often learned by heart. This was in spite of the church's persecution, which included official burnings of most of those New Testaments and sometimes their owners. Only three copies of this 1526 'Worms' New Testament survive.

Somewhere in Germany, Tyndale learned Hebrew (perhaps while he was in Worms, as it was a rabbinical centre). Hebrew was a language unknown in England beyond two antiquarian scholars in Cambridge. In 1530, from a printer in the flourishing port of Antwerp, Tyndale's English translations, again pocket size, of *The Five Books of Moses* (the Pentateuch) were smuggled over the sea. These were as eagerly received as his New Testaments, and as ruthlessly hunted. These five books were, in a sense, even more revealing: English readers had, for the first time, the name of God in English – Jehovah. And Tyndale had a special skill in getting Hebrew narrative into English: it is no exaggeration to say that in that he has hardly been bettered.

In Antwerp in 1534, he printed his revision of his New Testament. He used his knowledge of Hebrew to illuminate the Greek, of St Paul especially. His revised New Testaments circulated widely, and more have survived, including one in the British Library owned, and marked, by Queen Anne Boleyn. It is this revision, now with valuable prefaces, especially a long one to the Epistle to the Romans, and a few brief helpful notes on each page, that went forward to be the basis of all versions that followed. (It is worth observing that Tyndale is still censured, by those who have not read him, for his 'many violent anti-Catholic marginal notes'. These are a myth. The margins of the 1534 New Testament briefly explicate the text, or signal the place, often in one word, as 'Babes' or 'Leaven'. That is all.)

In the summer of 1535, while he was continuing his Old Testament translation, and living safely, as he thought, in the English House in Antwerp, he was tricked by a villainous Englishman, Henry Phillips, who was paid for ensuring Tyndale's arrest and ultimate death. Officially charged with being a heretic, Tyndale was cast into a cell in Vilvoorde Castle outside Brussels. He spent sixteen months there, without light in the evenings, his request for his own warm clothing and books ignored. He was interrogated by senior prosecuting scholars from the new Catholic University of Leuven, and condemned. Outside the castle, on the morning of 6 October 1536, having been publicly degraded from the priesthood, Tyndale was tied to a stake and garrotted. His body was burned. That he was not, as heretics had to be, burned alive, reflected his stature as a scholar. His last words were said to be 'Lord, open the King of England's eyes.' Henry VIII was already moving towards encouraging English Bibles, but these moves were too late to save Tyndale.

The chaplain to the English House, John Rogers, assembled all that Tyndale had translated and printed, and the unpublished manuscript of his translation of the next quarter of the Old Testament, the historical books from Joshua to 2 Chronicles. He arranged their publication in Antwerp in 1537 in a complete volume known, for reasons of security, as 'Thomas Matthew's Bible'. (Rogers took the second half of the Old Testament, which Tyndale had not reached, from the 1535 Antwerp translation made by Miles Coverdale, not from the Hebrew.)

'Matthew's Bible' circulated freely in England less than twelve months after Tyndale's execution. It was absorbed into new work by Coverdale, the 'Great Bible', issued in 1539 at the direction of the King, and to be placed in every one of the nine thousand parishes in England, with Erasmus's *Paraphrases of the New Testament* alongside. More significantly, Tyndale's work was the basis of, first, a New Testament translated and printed in Geneva in 1557, made by exiles from the persecution under Queen Mary Tudor: and then the similarly made 'Geneva Bible' of 1560. The latter was a work of great distinction: in the quality of printing, in the comprehensive aids to study in notes, essays, illustrations and maps, but above all in the now-forgotten achievement of the handful of men who made that volume, especially in translating for the first time into English, and well, the second half of the Old Testament, the difficult part, all of it being poetry.

The Geneva New Testament was revised in 1576, and new notes on Revelation were added in 1599. Before it was pushed out for political and commercial reasons in the mid-seventeenth century, by the new 'King James' Bible of 1611, 'Geneva' was the Bible of the nation, with a million copies bought between 1560 and 1640. (Again, it has to be stressed that the common condemnation of Geneva Bibles, handed down by writers who have never held a copy, that they are full of a Calvinism that was quite unacceptable in Elizabethan and Jacobean England, is both false to those Bibles and misunderstands the age. Similarly, a parallel observation, often repeated, again made by those who have never studied those Bibles, about the 'virulent anti-Catholic marginal notes' in all Geneva Bibles, is another myth. It is true that occasional marginal notes added to the Book of Revelation in some Geneva Bibles from 1599 attack some older popes; pontiffs like Gregory VII, and Gregory IX, and 'Boniface the eight', who was so hated by Dante that he placed him upside down in a subterranean furnace in hell. But the wholesale hatred of Catholics in Geneva Bibles, so frequently canvassed, is, like the total immersion in Calvinism, simply not there.)

The success of 'Geneva' was in spite of there being, as well as the 'King James', two other rivals: the Bishops Bible (1568), in which the Hebrew work was poor, and the Catholic Rheims New Testament (1582), followed by the whole Catholic Douai Bible (1610). Those were both marked by prologues and notes expressing intemperate hostility to 'the Heretics', by which words they mean Tyndale and his successors: neither publication had any significant impact on English life. (The frequent statement that King James's revisers relied heavily on the Rheims New Testament is not borne out by study of the matter.)

Even a partly diligent student can follow Tyndale's Bible work from his first editions between 1526 and 1534, and the Old Testament historical books in 1537, right through all later versions: even, silently, in what one may, this time correctly, call 'the violently Catholic' Rheims New Testament. The Bible passages given below will be evidence of Tyndale's enduring skills.

TYNDALE'S OTHER WORKS

In Cologne in 1525, Tyndale's first English New Testament was abandoned when only the first Gospel was set up in print, and not all of that. He had, however, written a Prologue, the sheets of which, smuggled into England, made the first printed Lutheran document to be circulated there. It is a translation of Luther's

Prologue to his 1522 German New Testament in English, a little cut and then expanded by Tyndale himself. This 'Cologne fragment' survives in one copy in the British Library.

One copy also remains, in the Bodleian Library, of Tyndale's slim, small book, also printed in Worms, and to accompany his 1526 New Testament, his *A Compendious Introduction to Romans, with a Treatise on the Paternoster*. In this, the second Protestant tract in English, Tyndale feels freer to weave in and out of Luther. He is translating Luther's Prologue to Romans in all his New Testaments, a document of the greatest significance to all European reformers, expounding Paul's doctrine of justification by faith rather than works.

Four or five years later, in about 1530, Tyndale again expanded the Prologue to his Cologne fragment to make a short book, *A Pathway to the Holy Scripture*. It was intended as a guide to the New Testament, again to be read alongside his 1526 Worms New Testament. Now less dependent on Luther, Tyndale again expounds the central doctrines of Paul in Romans.

Tyndale published most of his books in Antwerp. Two printed there in 1528 were immediately banned in England as heretical. To modern readers mysteriously titled, *The Parable of the Wicked Mammon* expounds the parable in Luke 16, more familiarly known as that of the Unjust Steward. 'Mammon' is riches, and Tyndale shows the New Testament teaching that though good works are important, they come naturally only from true faith, as fruit comes from the tree. Over-emphasis on works leads only to superstition.

In spite of the ban, and the fifty-four articles of heresy declared to be found in it by the bishops, his second book of 1528, *The Obedience of a Christian Man*, was especially influential. Enemies of reform, and Thomas More in particular, were asserting that the reformers throughout Europe were encouraging sedition and teaching treason. Tyndale wrote to explain that this was a lie. He declared for the first time the two fundamental principles of English reformers: the supreme authority of scripture in the church, and the supreme authority of the king in the state. Tyndale makes many pages of his book out of scripture, defending the right of all Christians to read the Word of God in their own language. He is scalding about the corruptions and superstitions caused by monks and friars, and sees the whole church bureaucracy, from the pope down, 'selling for money what God in Christ promiseth freely'. His attacks on the follies of the rival metaphysical schools of theology make exhilarating reading. Humble men and women were interrogated, and burned, for possessing this book: Anne Boleyn showed her copy to her royal husband-to-be, who delighted in it and declared that 'this is a book for me and all kings to read'.

Tyndale's short *The Practice of Prelates* was published in Antwerp in 1531. In it he takes up the old image of the pope's conspiracy as ivy strangling the English nation's tree ('practice' carries also the older meaning of trickery). His central attack is on Thomas Wolsey, and what he sees as the international forces at work in that Cardinal's upward climb. Tyndale argues for the presence of conspiracy in the support for King Henry's divorce of Catherine, which in some pages he learnedly opposes, to the anger of the King: the pages were removed in editions of the time.

In 1531, Tyndale answered the full-length attack, More's *Dialogue Concerning Heresies* (1529), with his own shorter *An Answer unto sir Thomas More's Dialogue*. At root, More's intemperately expressed objections amounted to no more than his offence that Tyndale had given the people Paul in English, and translated key New Testament words in their Greek sense, as 'congregation', 'love', and 'repent', in stead of the church's 'church', 'charity' and 'do penance'.

His little book was the end of the matter for Tyndale. Not so for More. He responded to Tyndale with his enormous *Confutation of Tyndale's Answer* (1532–3), half a million words, almost two thousand heavy pages, in six books and still unfinished at his death. Almost every page of the first five books pillories Tyndale, 'a new Judas', 'worse than Sodom and Gomorrah', 'a hell-hound in the kennel of the devil', 'discharging a filthy foam of blasphemies out of his brutish beastly mouth', and so on. More returned to the attack in other books.

Tyndale in 1531 published *An Exposition upon the First Epistle of John*, a section-by-section unfolding of that book, quiet in tone, but enjoying a passage of mockery of the worship of saints and images, expounding John's 'Little children, beware of images', as he translates John's concluding words. Early in 1533 came Tyndale's *Exposition upon the V, VI, VII chapter of Matthew* (that is, the Sermon on the Mount). Here Tyndale contrasts the work of Christ in restoring the true meaning of God's commandments – works resulting from faith – with many corrupt practices of the church. Tyndale's *A brief declaration of the sacraments* seems not to have been published until 1548. In it, Tyndale argues that it is the inner faith of the communicant which makes the sacrament of the Lord's Supper. This doctrine More furiously denied: for holding it, More ensured the arrest, torture and burning of John Frith. It has for four hundred and fifty years been the central doctrine of the Church of England. (The Supper of the Lord, also powerfully attacked by More, was not, as he believed it was, by Tyndale.) Tyndale also wrote, but did not publish, an essay on the will of William Tracy, in which Tracy declared his trust to be saved by the merits of Christ and not by works, for which 'heresy' his body was dug up and burned.

Not reconstructed until 1966, Tyndale's defence in prison in the face of his Leuven inquisitors was entitled either *Sola Fides justificat apud Deum* ('faith alone justifies before God') or, as is more likely, *Clavis intelligentiae salutaris sacrae scripturae* ('the key to the understanding of scripture as salvation').

TYNDALE'S LEGACY

The bed-rock of the Bible in English is a language of great clarity and accuracy, which always speaks directly to the heart. Tyndale set the standard in the 1520s and 1530s against which all later versions, now amounting to several thousands, have to be measured. His Greek was excellent. Hebrew scholars find his Old Testament translations remarkable for their understanding of the original. His craftsmanship with the English language amounted to genius.

These qualities matter. When we find a modern New Testament translation telling us that after his betrayal of Jesus, Peter went out and 'cried hard', we turn to Tyndale to find 'wept bitterly', wondering why it was ever necessary to change. Not only does Tyndale there translate the Greek correctly: the rhythm of his two words carries the experience. When we find in another modern version St Paul in 1 Corinthians 13 writing 'It won't be long before the weather clears and the sun shines bright!' again we turn to Tyndale for the haunting, and accurate to the Greek, 'then shall I know even as I am known', words describing experience of God through love; words which went on into the 'King James' 1611 version and far beyond.

Even beyond those solid, everlasting gifts to Bibles in English, accuracy and clarity, Tyndale's craftsmanship in making English sentences, out of Greek and Hebrew, and writing on his own, can amount – in his vocabulary, in his sense of rhythm and cadence – to a work of genius. Writing to readers at the beginning of his *Obedience*, about the hatred of Jesus by the officially religious, he concludes the passage with the Gospel story in a nutshell:

> Finally when they had done all they could and that they thought sufficient, and when Christ was in the heart of the earth and so many bills and poleaxes about him, to keep him down, and when it was past man's help: the holp God. When man could not bring him again, God's truth fetched him again.

A NOTE ON THE TEXT

The texts used in this collection are: *Tyndale's New Testament* (New Haven and London: Yale University Press, 1995) and *Tyndale's Old Testament* (New Haven and London: Yale University Press, 1992), *William Tyndale: The Obedience of a Christian Man* (Penguin Classics, 2000), and the three volumes of Tyndale's *Doctrinal Treatises et al.* (Cambridge: Cambridge University Press, for the Parker Society, 1848–50), with punctuation corrected.

Conventions for Biblical and other references have not generally been made consistent between texts, but left as in the originals.

From *Tyndale's New Testament*, 1534

THE GOSPEL OF ST MATTHEW

Chapter Two

When Jesus was born at Bethlehem in Jewry, in the time of Herod the king, behold, there came wise men from the east to Jerusalem saying: Where is he that is born king of the Jews? We have seen his star in the east, and are come to worship him.

When Herod the king had heard this, he was troubled, and all Jerusalem with him, and he gathered all the chief priests and scribes of the people, and asked of them where Christ should be born. And they said unto him: at Bethlehem in Jewry. For thus it is written by the prophet. And thou Bethlehem in the land of Jewry, art not the least concerning the princes of Juda. For out of thee shall come the captain, that shall govern my people Israel.

Then Herod privily called the wise men, and diligently enquired of them, the time of the star that appeared, and sent them to Bethlehem saying: Go and search diligently for the child. And when ye have found him, bring me word, that I may come and worship him also.

When they had heard the king, they departed: and lo the star which they saw in the east, went before them, till it came and stood over the place where the child was. When they saw the star, they were marvellously glad: and went into the house, and found the child with Mary his mother, and kneeled down and worshipped him, and opened their treasures, and offered unto him gifts, gold, frankincense and myrrh. And after they were warned of God in a dream, that they should not go again to Herod, they returned into their own country another way.

When they were departed: behold the angel of the Lord appeared to Joseph in dream saying: arise, and take the child and his mother, and fly into Egypt, and abide there till I bring thee word. For Herod will seek the child to destroy him. Then he arose, and took the child and his mother by night, and departed into Egypt, and was there unto the death of Herod, to fulfil that which

1

was spoken of the Lord, by the prophet which saith, out of Egypt have I called my son.

Then Herod perceiving that he was mocked of the wise men, was exceeding wroth, and sent forth and slew all the children that were in Bethlehem, and in all the coasts thereof, as many as were two year old and under, according to the time which he had diligently searched out of the wise men.

Then was fulfilled that which was spoken by the prophet Jeremy saying: On the hills was a voice heard, mourning, weeping, and great lamentation: Rachel weeping for her children, and would not be comforted, because they were not.

When Herod was dead: behold, an angel of the Lord appeared in a dream to Joseph in Egypt saying: arise and take the child and his mother, and go into the land of Israel. For they are dead which sought the child's life. Then he arose up, and took the child and his mother, and came into the land of Israel. But when he heard that Archelaus did reign in Jewry, in the room of his father Herod, he was afraid to go thither. Notwithstanding after he was warned of God in a dream, he turned aside into the parts of Galilee, and went and dwelt in a city called Nazareth, to fulfil that which was spoken by the prophets: he shall be called a Nazarite.

Chapter Five

When he saw the people, he went up into a mountain, and when he was set, his disciples came to him, and he opened his mouth, and taught them saying: Blessed are the poor in spirit: for theirs is the kingdom of heaven. Blessed are they that mourn: for they shall be comforted. Blessed are the meek: for they shall inherit the earth. Blessed are they which hunger and thirst for righteousness: for they shall be filled. Blessed are the merciful: for they shall obtain mercy. Blessed are the pure in heart: for they shall see God. Blessed are the peacemakers: for they shall be called the children of God. Blessed are they which suffer persecution for righteousness' sake: for theirs is the kingdom of heaven. Blessed are ye when men revile you, and persecute you, and shall falsely say all manner of evil sayings against you for my sake. Rejoice, and be glad, for great is your reward in heaven. For so persecuted they the prophets which were before your days.

Ye are the salt of the earth: but and if the salt have lost her saltness, what can be salted therewith? It is thenceforth good for nothing, but to be cast out, and to be trodden under foot of men. Ye are the light of the world. A city that is set on an hill, cannot be hid, neither do men light a candle and put it under a bushel, but on a candlestick, and it lighteth all that are in the house. Let your light so shine before men, that they may see your good works, and glorify your father which is in heaven.

Think not that I am come to destroy the law, or the prophets: no I am not come to destroy them, but to fulfil them. For truly I say unto you, till heaven and earth perish, one jot or one tittle of the law shall not scape, till all be fulfilled.

Whosoever breaketh one of these least commandments, and teacheth men so, he shall be called the least in the kingdom of heaven. But whosoever observeth and teacheth, the same shall be called great in the kingdom of heaven.

For I say unto you, except your righteousness exceed the righteousness of the scribes and Pharisees, ye cannot enter into the kingdom of heaven.

Ye have heard how it was said unto them of the old time: Thou shalt not kill. For whosoever killeth, shall be in danger of judgement. But I say unto you, whosoever is angry with his brother, shall be in danger of judgement. Whosoever sayeth unto his brother Raca, shall be in danger of a council. But whosoever sayeth thou fool, shall be in danger of hell fire.

Therefore when thou offerest thy gift at the altar, and there rememberest that thy brother hath ought against thee: leave there thine offering before the altar, and go thy way first and be reconciled to thy brother, and then come and offer thy gift.

Agree with thine adversary quickly, whiles thou art in the way with him, lest that adversary deliver thee to the judge, and the judge deliver thee to the minister, and then thou be cast into prison. I say unto thee verily: thou shalt not come out thence till thou have paid the utmost farthing.

Ye have heard how it was said to them of old time: Thou shalt not commit advoutry. But I say unto you, that whosoever looketh on a wife, lusting after her, hath committed advoutry with her already in his heart.

Wherefore if thy right eye offend thee, pluck him out, and cast him from thee. Better it is for thee that one of thy members perish, than that thy whole body should be cast into hell. Also if thy right hand offend thee, cut him off and cast him from thee. Better it is

3

that one of thy members perish, than that all thy body should be cast into hell.

It is said, whosoever put away his wife, let him give her a testimonial also of the divorcement. But I say unto you: whosoever put away his wife, (except it be for fornication) causeth her to break matrimony. And whosoever marrieth her that is divorced, breaketh wedlock.

Again ye have heard how it was said to them of old time, thou shalt not forswear thyself, but shalt perform thine oath to God. But I say unto you, swear not at all: neither by heaven, for it is God's seat: nor yet by the earth, for it is his footstool: neither by Jerusalem, for it is the city of that great king: neither shalt thou swear by thy head, because thou canst not make one white hair, or black: But your communication shall be, yea, yea: nay, nay. For whatsoever is more than that, cometh of evil.

Ye have heard how it is said, an eye for an eye: a tooth for a tooth. But I say to you, that ye resist not wrong. But whosoever give thee a blow on thy right cheek, turn to him the other. And if any man will sue thee at the law, and take away thy coat, let him have thy cloak also. And whosoever will compel thee to go a mile, go with him twain. Give to him that asketh, and from him that would borrow turn not away.

Ye have heard how it is said: thou shalt love thine neighbour, and hate thine enemy. But I say unto you, love your enemies. Bless them that curse you. Do good to them that hate you. Pray for them which do you wrong and persecute you, that ye may be the children of your father that is in heaven: for he maketh his sun to arise on the evil, and on the good, and sendeth his rain on the just and unjust. For if ye love them, which love you: what reward shall ye have? Do not the publicans even so? And if ye be friendly to your brethren only: what singular thing do ye? Do not the publicans likewise? Ye shall therefore be perfect, even as your father which is in heaven, is perfect.

Chapter Six

Take heed to your alms, that ye give it not in the sight of men, to the intent that ye would be seen of them. Or else ye get no reward of your father which is in heaven. Whensoever therefore thou givest thine alms, thou shalt not make a trumpet to be blown before thee, as the hypocrites do in the synagogues and in the streets, for to be praised of men. Verily I say unto you, they have their reward. But when thou doest thine alms, let not thy left hand know, what thy right hand doth, that thine alms may be secret: and thy father which seeth in secret, shall reward thee openly.

And when thou prayest, thou shalt not be as the hypocrites are. For they love to stand and pray in the synagogues, and in the corners of the streets, because they would be seen of men. Verily I say unto you, they have their reward. But when thou prayest, enter into thy chamber, and shut thy door to thee, and pray to thy father which is in secret: and thy father which seeth in secret, shall reward thee openly.

And when ye pray, babble not much, as the heathen do: for they think that they shall be heard, for their much babbling's sake. Be ye not like them therefore. For your father knoweth whereof ye have need, before ye ask of him. After this manner therefore pray ye.

O our father which art in heaven, hallowed be thy name. Let thy kingdom come. Thy will be fulfilled, as well in earth, as it is in heaven. Give us this day our daily bread. And forgive us our trespasses, even as we forgive our trespassers. And lead us not into temptation: but deliver us from evil. For thine is the kingdom and the power, and the glory for ever. Amen. For and if ye shall forgive other men their trespasses, your heavenly father shall also forgive you. But and ye will not forgive men their trespasses, no more shall your father forgive your trespasses.

Moreover when ye fast, be not sad as the hypocrites are. For they disfigure their faces, that they might be seen of men how they fast. Verily I say unto you, they have their reward. But thou, when thou fastest, anoint thine head, and wash thy face, that it appear not unto men how that thou fastest: but unto thy father which is in secret: and thy father which seeth in secret, shall reward thee openly.

See that ye gather you not treasure upon the earth, where rust and moths corrupt, and where thieves break through and steal. But gather ye treasure together in heaven, where neither rust nor moths corrupt, and where thieves neither break up nor yet steal. For wheresoever your treasure is, there will your hearts be also.

The light of the body is thine eye. Wherefore if thine eye be single, all thy body shall be full of light. But and if thine eye be wicked then all thy body shall be full of darkness. Wherefore if the light that is in thee, be darkness: how great is that darkness.

No man can serve two masters. For either he shall hate the one and love the other: or else he shall lean to the one and despise the other: ye cannot serve God and mammon. Therefore I say unto you, be not careful for your life, what ye shall eat, or what ye shall drink, nor yet for your body, what ye shall put on. Is not the life more worth than meat, and the body more of value than raiment? Behold the fowls of the air: for they sow not, neither reap, nor yet carry into the barns: and yet your heavenly father feedeth them. Are ye not much better than they?

Which of you (though he took thought therefore) could put one cubit unto his stature? And why care ye then for raiment? Consider the lilies of the field, how they grow. They labour not neither spin. And yet for all that I say unto you, that even Solomon in all his royalty was not arrayed like unto one of these.

Wherefore if God so clothe the grass, which is today in the field, and tomorrow shall be cast into the furnace: shall he not much more do the same unto you, o ye of little faith?

Therefore take no thought saying: what shall we eat, or what shall we drink, or wherewith shall we be clothed? After all these things seek the Gentiles. For your heavenly father knoweth that ye have need of all these things. But rather seek ye first the kingdom of heaven and the righteousness thereof, and all these things shall be ministered unto you.

Care not then for the morrow, but let the morrow care for itself: for the day present hath ever enough of his own trouble.

Chapter Seven

Judge not, that ye be not judged. For as ye judge so shall ye be judged. And with what measure ye mete, with the same shall it be measured to you again. Why seest thou a mote in thy brother's eye, and perceivest not the beam that is in thine own eye? Or why sayest thou to thy brother: suffer me to pluck out the mote out of thine eye, and behold a beam is in thine own eye. Hypocrite, first cast out the beam out of thine own eye, and then shalt thou see clearly to pluck out the mote out of thy brother's eye.

Give not that which is holy, to dogs, neither cast ye your pearls before swine, lest they tread them under their feet, and the other turn again and all to-rend you.

Ask and it shall be given you. Seek and ye shall find. Knock and it shall be opened unto you. For whosoever asketh receiveth and he that seeketh findeth, and to him that knocketh, it shall be opened. Is there any man among you which if his son asked him bread, would offer him a stone? Or if he asked fish, would he proffer him a serpent? If ye then which are evil, can give to your children good gifts: how much more shall your father which is in heaven, give good things to them that ask him?

Therefore whatsoever ye would that men should do to you, even so do ye to them. This is the law and the prophets.

Enter in at the strait gate: for wide is the gate, and broad is the way that leadeth to destruction: and many there be which go in thereat. But strait is the gate, and narrow is the way which leadeth unto life: and few there be that find it.

Beware of false prophets, which come to you in sheep's clothing but inwardly they are ravening wolves. Ye shall know them by their fruits. Do men gather grapes of thorns? Or figs of briars? Even so every good tree bringeth forth good fruit. But a corrupt tree, bringeth forth evil fruit. A good tree cannot bring forth bad fruit: nor yet a bad tree can bring forth good fruit. Every tree that bringeth not forth good fruit, shall be hewn down, and cast into the fire. Wherefore by their fruits ye shall know them.

Not all they that say unto me, Master, Master, shall enter in to the kingdom of heaven: but he that doth my father's will which is in heaven. Many will say to me in that day, Master, master, have we not in thy name prophesied? And in thy name have cast out devils? And in thy name have done many miracles? And then will I knowledge unto them, that I never knew them. Depart from me, ye workers of iniquity.

Whosoever heareth of me these sayings and doeth the same, I will liken him unto a wise man which built his house on a rock: and abundance of rain descended, and the floods came, and the winds blew and beat upon that same house, and it fell not, because it was grounded on the rock. And whosoever heareth of me these sayings and doeth them not, shall be likened unto a foolish man which built his house upon the sand: and abundance of rain descended, and the floods came, and the winds blew and beat upon that house, and it fell, and great was the fall of it.

And it came to pass, that when Jesus had ended these sayings, the people were astonied at his doctrine. For he taught them as one having power, and not as the scribes.

THE GOSPEL OF ST LUKE

from *Chapter Two*

And it chanced in those days: that there went out a commandment from August the Emperor, that all the world should be taxed. And this taxing was the first and executed when Cyrenius was lieutenant in Syria. And every man went unto his own city to be taxed. And Joseph also ascended from Galilee, out of a city called Nazareth, into Jewry: unto the city of David which is called Bethlehem, because he was of the house and lineage of David, to be taxed with Mary his spoused wife which was with child.

And it fortuned while they were there, her time was come that she should be delivered. And she brought forth her first begotten son, and wrapped him in swaddling clothes, and laid him in a manger, because there was no room for them within in the inn.

And there were in the same region shepherds abiding in the field and watching their flock by night. And lo: the angel of the Lord stood hard by them, and the brightness of the Lord shone round about them, and they were sore afraid. But the angel said unto them: Be not afraid. For behold, I bring you tidings of great joy that shall come to all the people: for unto you is born this day in the city of David, a saviour which is Christ the Lord. And take this for a sign: ye shall find the child swaddled and laid in a manger. And straightway there was with the angel a multitude of heavenly soldiers, lauding God and saying: Glory to God on high, and peace on the earth: and unto men rejoicing.

And it fortuned, as soon as the angels were gone away from them into heaven, the shepherds said one to another: let us go even unto Bethlehem, and see this thing that is happened which the Lord hath shewed unto us. And they came with haste, and found Mary and Joseph and the babe laid in a manger. And when they had seen it, they published abroad the saying which was told them of that child. And all that heard it, wondered at those things which were told them of the shepherds. But Mary kept all those sayings, and pondered them in her heart. And the shepherds returned, praising and lauding God for all that they had heard and seen, even as it was told unto them.

Chapter Fifteen

Then resorted unto him all the publicans and sinners, for to hear him. And the Pharisees and scribes murmured saying: He received to his company sinners, and eateth with them. Then put he forth this similitude to them saying: What man of you having an hundred sheep, if he lose one of them, doth not leave ninety and nine in the wilderness, and go after that which is lost, until he find him? And when he hath found him, he putteth him on his shoulders with joy: And as soon as he cometh home, he calleth together his lovers and neighbours saying unto them: rejoice with me, for I have found my sheep which was lost. I say unto you, that likewise joy shall be in heaven over one sinner that repenteth, more then over ninety and nine just persons, which need no repentance. Either what woman having ten groats, if she lose one, doth not light a candle, and sweep the house, and seek diligently, till she find it? And when she hath found it she calleth her lovers and her neighbours saying: Rejoice with me, for I have found the groat which I had lost. Likewise I say unto you, joy is made in the presence of the angels of God over one sinner that repenteth.

And he said: a certain man had two sons, and the younger of them said to his father: father, give me my part of the goods that to me belongeth. And he divided unto them his substance. And not long after, the younger son gathered all that he had together, and took his journey into a far country, and there he wasted his goods with riotous living. And when he had spent all that he had, there rose a great dearth throughout all that same land, and he began to lack. And he went and clave to a citizen of that same country, which sent him to his field, to keep his swine. And he would fain have filled his belly with the cods that the swine ate: and no man gave him.

Then he came to himself and said: how many hired servants at my father's, have bread enough, and I die for hunger. I will arise, and go to my father and will say unto him: father, I have sinned against heaven and before thee, and am no more worthy to be called thy son: make me as one of thy hired servants. And he arose and went to his father. And when he was yet a great way off, his father saw him and had compassion, and ran and fell on his neck, and kissed him. And the son said unto him: father, I have sinned against heaven, and in thy sight, and am no more worthy to be called thy son. But his father said to his servants: bring forth that best garment and put it on him, and put a ring on his hand, and shoes on his feet. And bring hither that fatted calf, and kill him, and let us eat and be merry: for this my son was dead, and is alive again, he was lost, and is now found. And they began to be merry.

The elder brother was in the field, and when he came and drew nigh to the house, he heard minstrelsy and dancing, and called one of his servants, and asked what those things meant. And he said unto him: thy brother is come, and thy father had killed the fatted calf, because he hath received him safe and sound. And he was angry, and would not go in. Then came his father out, and entreated him. He answered and said to his father: Lo these many years have I done thee service, neither brake at any time thy commandment, and yet gavest thou me never so much as a kid to make merry with my lovers: but as soon as this thy son was come, which hath devoured thy goods with harlots, thou hast for his pleasure killed the fatted calf. And he said unto him: Son, thou wast ever with me, and all that I have, is thine: it was meet that we should make merry and be glad: for this thy brother was dead, and is alive again: and was lost, and is found.

from *Chapter Sixteen*

There was a certain rich man, which was clothed in purple and fine byss, and fared deliciously every day. And there was a certain beggar, named Lazarus, which lay at his gate full of sores, desiring to be refreshed with the crumbs which fell from the rich man's board. Nevertheless, the dogs came and licked his sores. And it fortuned that the beggar died, and was carried by the angels into Abraham's bosom. The rich man also died, and was buried.

And being in hell in torments, he lift up his eyes and saw Abraham afar off, and Lazarus in his bosom, and he cried and said: father Abraham, have mercy on me, and send Lazarus that he may dip the tip of his finger in water, and cool my tongue: for I am tormented in this flame. But Abraham said unto him, Son, remember that thou in thy lifetime, receivedst thy pleasure, and contrarywise Lazarus pain. Now therefore is he comforted, and thou art punished. Beyond all this, between you and us there is a great space set, so that they which would go from hence to you cannot: neither may come from thence to us.

Then he said: I pray thee therefore father, send him to my

father's house. For I have five brethren: for to warn them, lest they also come into this place of torment. Abraham said unto him: they have Moses and the prophets, let them hear them. And he said: nay father Abraham, but if one came unto them, from the dead, they would repent. He said unto him: If they hear not Moses and the prophets, neither will they believe, though one rose from death again.

from *Chapter Eighteen*

And he put forth this similitude, unto certain which trusted in themselves that they were perfect, and despised other. Two men went up into the temple to pray: the one a Pharisee, and the other a publican. The Pharisee stood and prayed thus with himself. God I thank thee that I am not as other men are, extortioners, unjust, advoutrers, or as this publican. I fast twice in the week. I give tithe of all that I possess. And the publican stood afar off, and would not lift up his eyes to heaven, but smote his breast saying: God be merciful to me a sinner. I tell you: this man departed home to his house justified more than the other. For every man that exalteth himself, shall be brought low: And he that humbleth himself, shall be exalted.

Chapter Twenty-Four

On the morrow after the sabbath, early in the morning, they came unto the tomb and brought the odours which they had prepared and other women with them. And they found the stone rolled away from the sepulchre, and went in: but found not the body of the Lord Jesus. And it happened, as they were amazed thereat, behold two men stood by them in shining vestures. And as they were afraid, and bowed down their faces to the earth, they said to them: why seek ye the living among the dead? He is not here: but is risen. Remember how he spake unto you, when he was yet with you in Galilee, saying: that the son of man must be delivered into the hands of sinful men, and be crucified, and the third day rise again.

And they remembered his words, and returned from the sepulchre, and told all these things unto the eleven, and to all the remnant. It was Mary Magdalene and Joanna, and Mary Jacobi, and other that were with them, which told these things unto the apostles, and their words seemed unto them feigned things, neither believed they them. Then arose Peter and ran unto the sepulchre, and stooped in and saw the linen clothes laid by themself, and departed wondering in himself at that which had happened.

And behold, two of them went that same day to a town which was from Jerusalem about three score furlongs, called Emmaus: and they talked together of all these things that had happened. And it chanced, as they communed together and reasoned, that Jesus himself drew near, and went with them. But their eyes were holden, that they could not know him. And he said unto them: What manner of communications are these that ye have one to another as ye walk, and are sad? And the one of them named Cleopas, answered and said unto him: art thou only a stranger in Jerusalem, and hast not known the things which have chanced therein in these days? To whom he said: what things?

And they said unto him: of Jesus of Nazareth which was a prophet, mighty in deed, and word, before God, and all the people. And how the high priests, and our rulers delivered him to be condemned to death: and have crucified him. But we trusted that it should have been he that should have delivered Israel. And as touching all these things, today is even the third day, that they were done.

Yea, and certain women also of our company made us astonied, which came early unto the sepulchre, and found not his body: and came saying, that they had seen a vision of angels, which said that he was alive. And certain of them which were with us, went their way to the sepulchre, and found it even so as the women had said: but him they saw not.

And he said unto them: O fools and slow of heart to believe all that the prophets have spoken. Ought not Christ to have suffered these things, and to enter into his glory? And he began at Moses, and at all the prophets, and interpreted unto them in all scriptures which were written of him. And they drew nigh unto the town which they went to. And he made as though he would have gone further. But they constrained him saying: abide with us, for it draweth towards night, and the day is far passed. And he went in to tarry with them.

And it came to pass as he sat at meat with them, he took bread, blessed it, brake and gave to them. And their eyes were opened, and they knew him: and he vanished out of their sight. And they said between themselves: did not our hearts burn within us, while he talked with us by the way, and as he opened to us the scriptures? And they rose up the same hour, and returned again to Jerusalem, and found the eleven gathered together and them that were with them, which said: the Lord is risen indeed and hath appeared to Simon. And they told what things was done in the way, and how they knew him in breaking of bread.

As they thus spake Jesus himself stood in the midst of them, and said unto them: peace be with you. And they were abashed and afraid, supposing that they had seen a spirit. And he said unto them: Why are ye troubled, and why do thoughts arise in your hearts? Behold my hands and my feet, that it is even myself. Handle me and see: for spirits have not flesh and bones, as ye see me have. And when he had thus spoken, he shewed them his hands and his feet. And while they yet believed not for joy, and wondered, he said unto them: Have ye here any meat? And they gave him a piece of a broiled fish, and of an honeycomb. And he took it, and ate it before them.

And he said unto them. These are the words, which I spake unto you, while I was yet with you: that all must be fulfilled which were written of me in the law of Moses, and in the Prophets, and in the Psalms. Then opened he their wits, that they might understand the scriptures, and said unto them, Thus is it written, and thus it behoved Christ to suffer, and to rise again from death the third day, and that repentance and remission of sins should be preached in his name among all nations, and must begin at Jerusalem. And ye are witnesses of these things. And behold, I will send the promise of my father upon you. But tarry ye in the city of Jerusalem, until ye be endued with power from on high.

And he led them out into Bethany, and lift up his hands, and blest them. And it came to pass, as he blessed them, he departed from them, and was carried up into heaven. And they worshipped him, and returned to Jerusalem with great joy, and were continually in the temple, praising and lauding God. Amen.

Here endeth the Gospel of Saint Luke.

THE GOSPEL OF SAINT JOHN

Chapter Fourteen

And he said unto his disciples: Let not your hearts be troubled. Believe in God and believe in me. In my father's house are many mansions. If it were not so, I would have told you. I go to prepare a place for you. And if I go to prepare a place for you, I will come again, and receive you even unto myself, that where I am, there may ye be also. And whither I go ye know, and the way ye know.

Thomas said unto him: Lord we know not whither thou goest. Also how is it possible for us to know the way? Jesus said unto him: I am the way, the truth and the life. And no man cometh unto the father, but by me. If ye had known me, ye had known my father also. And now ye know him, and have seen him.

Philip said unto him: Lord shew us the father, and it sufficeth us. Jesus said unto him: have I been so long time with you: and yet hast thou not known me? Philip, he that hath seen me, hath seen the father. And how sayest thou then: shew us the father? Believest thou not that I am in the father, and the father in me? The words that I speak unto you, I speak not of myself: but the father that dwelleth in me, is he that doeth the works. Believe me, that I am [in] the father and the father in me. At the least believe me for the very works' sake.

Verily verily I say unto you: he that believeth on me, the works that I do, the same shall he do, and greater works than these shall he do, because I go unto my father. And whatsoever ye ask in my name, that will I do, that the father might be glorified by the son. If ye shall ask any thing in my name, I will do it.

If ye love me keep my commandments, and I will pray the father, and he shall give you another comforter, that he may bide with you ever, which is the spirit of truth whom the world cannot receive, because the world seeth him not, neither knoweth him. But ye know him. For he dwelleth with you, and shall be in you. I will not leave you comfortless: but will come unto you.

Yet a little while and the world seeth me no more: but ye shall see me. For I live, and ye shall live. That day shall ye know that I am in my father, and you in me, and I in you.

He that hath my commandments and keepeth them, the same is he that loveth me. And he that loveth me, shall be loved of my father: and I will love him, and will shew mine own self unto him. Judas said unto him (not Judas Iscariot) Lord what is the cause that

14

thou wilt shew thyself unto us, and not unto the world? Jesus answered and said unto him: if a man love me and will keep my sayings, my father also will love him, and we will come unto him, and will dwell with him. He that loveth me not, keepeth not my sayings. And the words which ye hear, are not mine, but the father's which sent me.

This have I spoken unto you being yet present with you. But that comforter which is the holy ghost (whom my father will send in my name) he shall teach you all things, and bring all things to your remembrance whatsoever I have told you.

Peace I leave with you, my peace I give unto you. Not as the world giveth, give I unto you. Let not your hearts be grieved, neither fear ye. Ye have heard how I said unto you: I go and come again unto you. If ye loved me, ye would verily rejoice, because I said, I go unto the father. For the father is greater than I. And now have I showed you, before it come, that when it is come to pass, ye might believe.

Hereafter will I not talk many words unto you. For the ruler of this world cometh, and hath nought in me. But that the world may know that I love the father: therefore as the father gave me commandment, even so do I. Rise let us go hence.

THE EPISTLE OF ST PAUL TO THE ROMANS

Chapter Eight

There is then no damnation to them which are in Christ Jesus, which walk not after the flesh: but after the spirit. For the law of the spirit that bringeth life through Jesus Christ, hath delivered me from the law of sin and death. For what the law could not do inasmuch it was weak because of the flesh: that performed God, and sent his son in the similitude of sinful flesh, and by sin damned sin in the flesh: that the righteousness required of the law might be fulfilled in us, which walk not after the flesh, but after the spirit.

For they that are carnal, are carnally minded. But they that are spiritual, are ghostly minded. To be carnally minded, is death. But to be spiritually minded is life and peace. Because that the fleshly mind is enmity against God: for it is not obedient to the law of God, neither can be. So then they that are given to the flesh, cannot please God.

But ye are not given to the flesh, but to the spirit: if so be that the spirit of God dwell in you. If there be any man that hath not the spirit of Christ, the same is none of his. If Christ be in you, the body is dead because of sin: but the spirit is life for righteousness' sake. Wherefore if the spirit of him that raised up Jesus from death, dwell in you: even he that raised up Christ from death, shall quicken your mortal bodies, because that this spirit dwelleth in you.

Therefore brethren we are now debtors, not to the flesh, to live after the flesh. For if ye live after the flesh, ye must die. But if ye mortify the deeds of the body, by the help of the spirit, ye shall live. For as many as are led by the spirit of God: they are the sons of God. For ye have not received the spirit of bondage to fear any more, but ye have received the spirit of adoption whereby we cry Abba father. The same spirit certifieth our spirit that we are the sons of God. If we be sons, we are also heirs, the heirs I mean of God, and heirs annexed with Christ: if so be that we suffer together, that we may be glorified together.

For I suppose that the afflictions of this life, are not worthy of the glory which shall be showed upon us. Also the fervent desire of the creatures abideth looking when the sons of God shall appear, because the creatures are subdued to vanity against their will: but for his will which subdueth them in hope. For the very creatures shall be delivered from the bondage of corruption, into the glorious liberty of the sons of God. For we know that every creature groaneth with us also, and travaileth in pain even unto this time.

Not they only, but even we also which have the first fruits of the spirit, mourn in ourselves and wait for the adoption and look for the deliverance of our bodies. For we are saved by hope. But hope that is seen is no hope. For how can a man hope for that which he seeth? But and if we hope for that we see not, then do we with patience abide for it.

Likewise the spirit also helpeth our infirmities. For we know not what to desire as we ought: but the spirit maketh intercession mightily for us with groanings which cannot be expressed with tongue. And he that searcheth the hearts, knoweth what is the meaning of the spirit: for he maketh intercession for the saints according to pleasure of God. For we know that all things work for the best unto them that love God, which also are called of purpose. For those which he knew before, he also ordained before, that they should be like fashioned unto the shape of his son, that he might be the first begotten son among many brethren. Moreover which he appointed before, them he also called. And which he called, them also he justified, which he justified, them he also glorified.

What shall we then say unto these things? If God be on our side: who can be against us? which spared not his own son, but gave him for us all: how shall he not with him give us all things also? Who shall lay anything to the charge of God's chosen? it is God that justifieth: who then shall condemn? it is Christ which is dead, yea rather which is risen again, which is also on the right hand of God, and maketh intercession for us.

Who shall separate us from the love of God? shall tribulation? or anguish? or persecution? or hunger? or nakedness? or peril? or sword? As it is written: For thy sake are we killed all day long, and are counted as sheep appointed to be slain. Nevertheless in all these things we overcome strongly through his help that loved us. Yea and I am sure that neither death, neither life, neither angels, nor rule, neither power, neither things present, neither things to come, neither height, neither lowth, neither any other creature shall be able to depart us from the love of God, showed in Christ Jesus our Lord.

THE FIRST EPISTLE OF ST PAUL TO THE CORINTHIANS

Chapter Thirteen

Though I spake with the tongues of men and angels, and yet had no love, I were even as sounding brass: or as a tinkling cymbal. And though I could prophesy, and understood all secrets, and all knowledge: yea, if I had all faith so that I could move mountains out of their places, and yet had no love, I were nothing. And though I bestowed all my goods to feed the poor, and though I gave my body even that I burned, and yet had no love, it profiteth me nothing.

Love suffereth long, and is courteous. Love envieth not. Love doth not frowardly, swelleth not, dealeth not dishonestly, seeketh not her own, is not provoked to anger, thinketh not evil, rejoiceth not in iniquity: but rejoiceth in the truth, suffereth all things, believeth all things, hopeth all things, endureth in all things.

Though that prophesying fail, or tongues shall cease, or knowledge vanish away, yet love falleth never away.

For our knowledge is imperfect, and our prophesying is imperfect. But when that which is perfect is come, then that which is imperfect shall be done away. When I was a child, I spake as a child, I understood as a child, I imagined as a child. But as soon as I was a man, I put away childishness. Now we see in a glass even in a dark speaking: but then shall we see face to face. Now I know imperfectly: but then shall I know even as I am known. Now abideth faith, hope, and love, even these three: but the chief of these is love.

from *Chapter Fifteen*

If Christ be preached how that he rose from death: how say some that are among you, that there is no resurrection from death? If there be no rising again from death: then is Christ not risen. If Christ be not risen, then is our preaching vain, and your faith is also in vain. Yea and we are found false witnesses of God. For we have testified of God, how that he raised up Christ, whom he raised not up, if it be so that the dead rise not up again. For if the dead rise not again, then is Christ not risen again. If it be so that Christ rose not, then is your faith in vain and yet are ye in your sins. And thereto they which are fallen asleep in Christ, are perished. If in this life only we believe on Christ, then are we of all men the miserablest.

But now is Christ risen from death, and is become the first fruits of them that slept. For by a man came death, and by a man came resurrection from death. For as by Adam all die: even so by Christ, shall all be made alive, and every man in his own order. The first is Christ, then they that are Christ's at his coming. Then cometh the end, when he hath delivered up the kingdom to God the father, when he hath put down all rule, authority and power. For he must reign till he have put all his enemies under his feet.

The last enemy that shall be destroyed is death. For he hath put all things under his feet. But when he saith, all things are put under him, it is manifest that he is excepted, which did put all things under him. When all things are subdued unto him: then shall the son also himself be subject unto him that put all things under him, that God may be all in all things.

THE EPISTLE OF ST PAUL TO THE EPHESIANS

Chapter One

Paul an apostle of Jesus Christ, by the will of God.

To the saints which are at Ephesus, and to them which believe on Jesus Christ.

Grace be with you and peace from God our father, and from the Lord Jesus Christ.

Blessed be God the father of our Lord Jesus Christ, which hath blessed us with all manner of spiritual blessing in heavenly things by Christ, according as he had chosen us in him, before the foundation of the world was laid, that we should be saints, and without blame before him, through love. And ordained us before through Jesus Christ to be heirs unto himself, according to the pleasure of his will, to the praise of the glory of his grace wherewith he hath made us accepted in the beloved.

By whom we have redemption through his blood even the forgiveness of sins, according to the riches of his grace, which grace he shed on us abundantly in all wisdom, and perceivance. And hath opened unto us the mystery of his will according to his pleasure, and purposed the same in himself to have it declared when the time were full come, that all things, both the things which are in heaven, and also the things which are in earth, should be gathered together, even in Christ: that is to say, in him in whom we are made heirs, and were thereto predestinate according to the purpose of him which worketh all things after the purpose of his own will: that we which before believed in Christ should be unto the praise of his glory.

In whom also ye (after that ye heard the word of truth, I mean the gospel of your salvation, wherein ye believed) were sealed with the holy spirit of promise, which is the earnest of our inheritance, to redeem the purchased possession and that unto the laud of his glory.

Wherefore even I (after that I heard of the faith which ye have in the Lord Jesus, and love unto all the saints) cease not to give thanks for you, making mention of you in my prayers, that the God of our Lord Jesus Christ and the father of glory, might give unto you the spirit of wisdom, and open to you the knowledge of himself, and lighten the eyes of your minds, that ye might know what that hope is, whereunto he hath called you, and what the riches of his glorious inheritance is upon the saints, and what is the exceeding greatness of his power to us-ward which believe according to the working of that his mighty power, which he wrought in Christ, when he raised him from death, and set him on his right hand in heavenly things, above all rule, power, and might and domination, and above all names that are named, not in this world only, but also in the world to come: and hath put all things under his feet, and hath made him above all things, the head of the congregation which is his body and the fulness of him that filleth all in all things.

From *Tyndale's Old Testament*, 1530 and 1537

THE FIRST BOOK OF MOSES CALLED GENESIS

from *Chapter One*

In the beginning God created heaven and earth. The earth was void and empty, and darkness was upon the deep, and the spirit of God moved upon the water.

Then God said: let there be light and there was light. And God saw the light that it was good: and divided the light from the darkness, and called the light day, and the darkness night: and so of the evening and morning was made the first day.

And God said: let there be a firmament between the waters, and let it divide the waters asunder. Then God made the firmament and parted the waters which were under the firmament, from the waters that were above the firmament: And it was so. And God called the firmament heaven. And so of the evening and morning was made the second day.

And God said, let the waters that are under heaven gather themselves unto one place, that the dry land may appear: And it came so to pass. And God called the dry land the earth and the gathering together of waters called he the sea. And God saw that it was good.

Chapter Three

But the serpent was subtler than all the beasts of the field which the Lord God had made, and said unto the woman. Ah sir, that God hath said, ye shall not eat of all manner trees in the garden. And the woman said unto the serpent, of the fruit of the trees in the garden we may eat, but of the fruit of the tree that is in the midst of the garden (said God) see that ye eat not, and see that ye touch it not: lest ye die.

Then said the serpent unto the woman: tush ye shall not die: But God doth know, that whensoever ye should eat of it, your eyes should be opened and ye should be as God and know both good and evil. And the woman saw that it was a good tree to eat of and lusty unto the eyes and a pleasant tree for to make wise. And took of the fruit of it and ate, and gave unto her husband also with her, and he ate. And the eyes of both of them were opened, that they understood how that they were naked. Then they sewed fig leaves together and made them aprons.

And they heard the voice of the Lord God as he walked in the garden in the cool of the day. And Adam hid himself and his wife also from the face of the Lord God, among the trees of the garden. And the Lord God called Adam and said unto him where art thou? And he answered: Thy voice I heard in the garden, but I was afraid because I was naked, and therefore hid myself. And he said: who told thee that thou wast naked? hast thou eaten of the tree, of which I bade thee that thou shouldest not eat? And Adam answered: The woman which thou gavest to bear me company, she took me of the tree, and I ate. And the Lord God said unto the woman: wherefore didest thou so? And the woman answered, the serpent deceived me and I ate.

And the Lord God said unto the serpent: because thou hast so done most cursed be thou of all cattle and of all beasts of the field: upon thy belly shalt thou go: and earth shalt thou eat all days of thy life. Moreover I will put hatred between thee and the woman, and between thy seed and her seed. And that seed shall tread thee on the head, and thou shalt tread it on the heel.

And unto the woman he said: I will surely increase thy sorrow and make thee oft with child, and with pain shalt thou be delivered: And thy lusts shall pertain unto thy husband and he shall rule thee.

And unto Adam he said: forasmuch as thou hast obeyed the voice of thy wife, and hast eaten of the tree of which I commanded thee saying: see thou eat not thereof: cursed be the earth for thy sake. In sorrow shalt thou eat thereof all days of thy life, and it shall bear thorns and thistles unto thee. And thou shalt eat the herbs of the field: In the sweat of thy face shalt thou eat bread, until thou return unto the earth whence thou wast taken: for earth thou art, and unto earth shalt thou return.

And Adam called his wife Heva, because she was the mother of all that liveth. And the Lord God made Adam and his wife garments of skins, and put them on them. And the Lord God said: lo, Adam is become as it were one of us, in knowledge of good and evil. But now lest he stretch forth his hand and take also of the tree of life and eat and live ever.

And the Lord God cast him out of the garden of Eden, to till the earth whence he was taken. And he cast Adam out, and set at the entering of the garden Eden, cherubin with a naked sword moving in and out, to keep the way to the tree of life.

Chapter Thirty-Seven

And Jacob dwelt in the land wherein his father was a stranger, that is to say in the land of Canaan. And these are the generations of Jacob: when Joseph was seventeen years old, he kept sheep with his brethren, and the lad was with the sons of Bilha and of Zilpha his father's wives. And he brought unto their father an evil saying that was of them. And Israel loved Joseph more than all his children, because he begat him in his old age, and he made him a coat of many colours.

When his brethren saw that their father loved him more than all his brethren, they hated him and could not speak one kind word unto him. Moreover Joseph dreamed a dream and told it his brethren: wherefore they hated him yet the more. And he said unto them: hear I pray you this dream which I have dreamed: Behold we were making sheaves in the field: and lo, my sheaf arose and stood upright, and yours stood round about and made obeisance to my sheaf. Then said his brethren unto him: what, shalt thou be our king or shalt thou reign over us? And they hated him yet the more, because of his dream and of his words.

And he dreamed yet another dream and told it his brethren saying: behold, I have had one dream more: methought the sun and the moon and eleven stars made obeisance to me. And when he had told it unto his father and his brethren, his father rebuked him and said unto him: what meaneth this dream which thou hast dreamed: shall I and thy mother and thy brethren come and fall on the ground before thee? And his brethren hated him, but his father noted the saying.

His brethren went to keep their father's sheep in Sichem, and Israel said unto Joseph: do not thy brethren keep in Sichem? come that I may send thee to them. And he answered here am I. And he said unto him: go and see whether it be well with thy brethren and the sheep, and bring me word again: And sent him out of the vale of Hebron, for to go to Sichem.

And a certain man found him wandering out of his way in the field, and asked him what he sought. And he answered: I seek my brethren, tell me I pray thee where they keep sheep. And the man said, they are departed hence, for I heard them say, let us go unto Dothan. Thus went Joseph after his brethren, and found them in Dothan.

And when they saw him afar off before he came at them, they took counsel against him, for to slay him, and said one to another, Behold this dreamer cometh, come now and let us slay him and cast him into some pit, and let us say that some wicked beast hath devoured him, and let us see what his dreams will come to.

When Ruben heard that, he went about to rid him out of their hands and said, let us not kill him. And Ruben said moreover unto them, shed not his blood, but cast him into this pit that is in the wilderness, and lay no hands upon him: for he would have rid him out of their hands and delivered him to his father again.

And as soon as Joseph was come unto his brethren, they stripped him out of his gay coat that was upon him, and they took him and cast him into a pit. But the pit was empty and had no water therein. And they sat them down to eat bread. And as they lift up their eyes and looked about, there came a company of Ismaelites from Gilead, and their camels laden with spicery, balm, and myrrh, and were going down into Egypt.

Then said Juda to his brethren, what availeth it that we slay our brother, and keep his blood secret? come on, let us sell him to the Ismaelites, and let not our hands be defiled upon him: for he is our brother and our flesh. And his brethren were content. Then as the Madianites merchant men passed by, they drew Joseph out of the pit and sold him unto the Ismaelites for twenty pieces of silver. And they brought him into Egypt.

And when Ruben came again unto the pit and found not Joseph there, he rent his clothes and went again unto his brethren saying: the lad is not yonder, and whither shall I go? And they took Joseph's coat and killed a goat, and dipped the coat in the blood. And they sent that gay coat and caused it to be brought unto their father and said: This have we found: see, whether it be thy son's coat or no. And he knew it saying: it is my son's coat: a wicked beast hath devoured him, and Joseph is rent in pieces. And Jacob rent his cloathes, and put sack-cloth about his loins, and sorrowed for his son a long season.

Then came all his sons and all his daughters to comfort him.

24

And he would not be comforted, but said: I will go down into the grave unto my son, mourning. And thus his father wept for him. And the Madianites sold him in Egypt unto Putiphar a lord of Pharao's: and his chief marshal.

From A PROLOGUE INTO THE FIFTH BOOK OF MOSES CALLED DEUTERONOMY

This is a book worthy to be read in day and night and never to be out of hands. For it is the most excellent of all the books of Moses. It is easy also and light and a very pure gospel that is to wete, a preaching of faith and love: deducing the love to God out of faith, and the love of a man's neighbour out of the love of God. Herein also thou mayst learn right meditation or contemplation, which is nothing else save the calling to mind and a repeating in the heart of the glorious and wonderful deeds of God, and of his terrible handling of his enemies and merciful entreating of them that come when he calleth them, which thing this book doth and almost nothing else.

THE SECOND BOOK OF SAMUEL

from *Chapter Eighteen*

Then said Ahimaaz the son of Sadock: let me run I pray thee, and bear the king tidings, how that the Lord hath judged him quit of the hands of all his enemies. And Joab said unto him: thou art no man to bear tidings today: thou shalt bear tidings another time: but today thou shalt bear none, because the king's son is dead. Then said Joab to Chusi: go and tell the king what thou hast seen. And Chusi bowed himself unto Joab and ran. Then said Ahimaaz the son of Sadock again to Joab: come what come will, let me run I pray thee after Chusi. And Joab said: wherefore shouldest thou run my son? for and thou run thou gettest no reward: well come what will let me run. And he said unto him: run. Then Ahimaaz ran by the plain and overran Chusi.

And David sat between the two gates. And the watchman went up to the roof over the gate unto the wall, and lifted up his eyes and saw: and behold, there came a man running alone. And the watchman called and told the king. And the king said: if he come alone, there is tidings in his mouth. And he came and drew nigh. And the watchman saw another man running, and called unto the porter and said: behold there cometh another running alone. And the king answered: he is also a tidings bringer. And the watchman said: methinketh the running of the foremost is like the running of Ahimaaz the son of Sadock. And the king said: he is a good man and cometh with good tidings. And Ahimaaz called and said to the king: good tidings, and bowed himself to the earth upon his face before the king and said: blessed be the Lord thy God which hath shut up all the men that lifted up their hands against my lord the king. And the king said: is the lad Absalom safe? And Ahimaaz answered I saw a great ado, when the king's servant Joab sent me thy servant. But I wot not what it was. And the king said: turn and stand here. And he turned and stood.

And behold Chusi came and said: tidings my lord the king, the Lord hath quit thee this day out of the hands of all that rose against thee. And the king said to Chusi: is the lad Absalom safe? And Chusi answered: the enemies of my lord the king and all that rise against thee, to have thee, be as thy lad is. And the king was moved and went up to a chamber over the gate and wept. And as he went thus he said: my son Absalom, my son, my son, my son Absalom, would to God I had died for thee Absalom, my son, my son.

THE FIRST BOOK OF THE KINGS

from *Chapter Eighteen*

Then Eliah said: as truly as the Lord of hosts liveth, before whom I stand: I will show myself unto him this day. And thereupon Abdiah went to Ahab and told him. And Ahab went against Eliah. And when Ahab saw Eliah, he said unto him: art thou he that troubleth Israel? And he said: it is not I that trouble Israel, but thou and thy father's house, in that ye have forsaken the commandments of the Lord and hast followed Baal. But now send and gather to me all Israel unto mount Carmel and the prophets of Baal four hundred and fifty, and the prophets of the groves four hundred, which eat of Jezebel's table. And Ahab sent for all the children of Israel, and gathered the prophets unto mount Carmel.

And Eliah came unto all the people and said: why halt ye

between two opinions? If the Lord be very God, follow him: or if Baal be he follow him. And the people answered him not one word. Then said Eliah unto the people: I only remain of the Lord's prophets, and Baal's prophets are four hundred and fifty. Let two oxen be given us, and let them choose the one and cut him in pieces and lay him on wood, and put no fire under. And I will dress the other and put him on wood, and will put no fire under. And call ye on the name of your god, and I will call on the name of the Lord. And then the god that answereth by fire, he is the very God.

And all the people said: it is well spoken. Then said Eliah unto the prophets of Baal, choose you an ox and dress him first (for ye are many) and call on the name of your god, but put no fire under. And they took the ox that was given them and dressed it, and called on the name of Baal from morning to noon saying: O Baal hear us. But there was no voice nor answer. And they leapt about the altar that they had made. And at noon Eliah mocked them and said: call loud (for he is a god: but he is talking, or occupied, or in the way, or haply he sleepeth) that he may awake. And they cried loud, and cut themselves, as their manner was, with knives and lances, till the blood flowed on them. And when midday was passed, they prophesied until it was time to offer. But there was neither voice nor answer nor any that regarded them.

Then Eliah said to all the folk: come to me. And all the people came to him. And he mended the altar of the Lord that was broken. And he took twelve stones according to the number of the twelve tribes of the sons of Jacob, unto whom the word of the Lord came saying: Israel shall be thy name. And with the stones he made an altar in the name of the Lord. And he made a gutter round about the altar, able to receive two pecks of corn. And he put the wood in order, and hewed the ox in pieces, and put him on the wood, and said: fill four pitchers with water and pour it on the sacrifice and on the wood. And he said: do so again. And they did so again. Then he said: do it the third time. And they did so the third time. And the water ran round about the altar, and the gutter was full of water also.

And when offering time was come, Eliah the prophet went to and said: Lord God of Abraham, Isaac and of Israel, let it be known this day, that thou art the god in Israel, and that I am thy servant, and that I do all these things at thy commandment. Hear me O Lord, hear me, that this people may know, that thou Lord art the God, and that thou hast turned their hearts backward. And there fell fire from the Lord and consumed the sacrifice and the wood and the stones and the dust, and licked up the water that was in the gutter. And when all the people saw that, they fell on their faces and said: the Lord he is God, the Lord he is God. Then said Eliah unto them, lay hands on the prophets of Baal, let not one of them escape. And when they had taken them, Eliah brought them down unto the brook Kison, and slew them there.

Then Eliah said unto Ahab, get thee up and eat and drink, for there is a sound of much rain. And when Ahab went up to eat and to drink, Eliah went up to the top of mount Carmel. And bowed himself to the earth, and put his face between his knees, and said to his servant: go up and look toward the sea. And he went up and looked, and said: here is nothing. And he said go again seven times. And the seventh time he said: behold, there ariseth a little cloud out of the sea, like the palm of a man's hand. Then he said: go and say to Ahab, put the horses in the chariot, and get thee down that the rain stop thee not. And within a little while, heaven was black with clouds and wind, and there was a great rain. And Ahab rode and went to Jezrahel. And the hand of the Lord was on Eliah, and he girded up his loins and ran before Ahab, till they came to Jezrahel.

from *Chapter Nineteen*

Eliah fleeing from Jezabel is nourished by the angel of God. He complaineth that he is left alone, and that they seek his life too. He is commanded to anoint Azahel, Jehu and Eliseus.

And Ahab told Jezabel, all that Eliah had done, and altogether how he had slain the prophets with the sword. Then Jezabel sent a messenger unto Eliah saying: so do God to me and so thereto, except I make thy soul like one of theirs, by tomorrow this time: when he saw that, he arose and went for his life, and came to Bersabe in Juda, and left his lad there. And he went a day's journey into the wilderness, and when he was come sat down under a juniper tree, and desired for his soul that he might die, and said, it is now enough O Lord, take my soul, for I am not better than my fathers.

And as he lay and slept under the juniper tree: behold, there came an angel and touched him, and said unto him: up and eat.

And he looked about him: and see, there was a loaf of broiled bread and a cruse of water at his head. And he ate and drank and laid him down again to sleep. And the angel of the Lord came again the second time and touched him, and said: up and eat, for thou hast a long journey to go. And he arose and did eat and drink and went in the strength of that meat forty days and forty nights, unto Horeb the mount of God, and entered there into a cave and lodged there all night.

And then the word of the Lord came to him and said what doest thou here, Eliah? And he answered: I have been thorough angry for the Lord God of hosts' sake. For the children of Israel have forsaken thy covenant, and have broken down thine altars and slain the prophets with the sword, and I only am left, and they seek my soul to have it too. And he said come out and stand before the Lord. And behold, the Lord went by and a mighty strong wind that rent the mountains and brake the rocks before him. But the Lord was not in the wind. And after the wind came an earthquake. But the Lord was not in the earthquake. And after the earthquake, came fire: but the Lord was not in the fire. And after the fire, came a small still voice. And when Eliah heard it, he covered his face with his mantle, and went out and stood in the mouth of the cave. And see, there came a voice unto him and said: what doest thou here Eliah? And he answered: I was jealous for the Lord God of hosts' sake: because the children of Israel have forsaken thine appointment and have cast down thine altars and slain thy prophets with the sword, and I only am left, and they seek my soul to have it. Then the Lord said unto him: go and turn thy way to the wilderness of Damasco, and go and anoint Hazael to be king of Siria. And Jehu the son of Namsi anoint to be king over Israel. And Eliseus the son of Saphat of Abel Mehulah anoint to be prophet in thy room. And whoso escapeth the sword of Hazael, him shall Jehu slay: and if any man escape the sword of Jehu, him shall Eliseus slay. And thereto I have left me seven thousand in Israel, of which never man bowed his knees unto Baal nor kissed him with his mouth.

THE SECOND BOOK OF THE KINGS

from *Chapter Four*

And it fortuned on a time that [Eliseus] came thither and turned into the chamber and lay there. Then he said to Gihezi his servant: call this Sunamite. And he called her, and she came before him. And Eliseus said to him, say to her I pray thee: see, thou hast made all this provision for us, what shall we do for thee? wouldest thou be spoken for to the king or to the captain of the host? And she said I dwell among mine own people. Then he said, what is to be done for her? And Gihezi said: verily she hath no child and her husband is old. And he said: call her. And he called her. And she came and stood at the door. Then he said: by such a time, as soon as the fruit can live, thou shalt embrace a son, and she said, Oh nay my Lord thou man of God, do not lie unto the handmaid. And the wife conceived and bare a son the same season that Eliseus had said unto her as soon as the fruit could have life.

And when the lad was great, it fell on a day, that he went out to his father to the harvest time. And there he complained unto his father, my head, my head. And his father said to a lad, carry him to his mother. And he took him and brought him to his mother. And he sat on her knees till noon, and then died. And she carried him up and laid him on the bed of the man of God, and shut the door to him, and went out, and came to her husband and said: send me one of the young men and an ass that I may run to the man of God. And he said: wherefore wilt thou go to him today, while it is neither new moon nor sabbath day? And she said: be content. Then she saddled an ass and said to the lad: lead away and make me not cease riding, until I bid thee.

And so she went and came unto the man of God, to mount Carmel. And when the man of God saw her afar, he said to Gihezi his servant: see, where our servant cometh. Now run against her, and ask her, whether it be all well with her, and with her husband and with the lad. And she said: all is well. Then she went to the man of God up to the hill and caught him by the feet. And Gihezi went to her, to thrust her away. But the man of God said: let her alone, for her soul is vexed, and the Lord hath hid it from me and hath not told it me. Then she said: did I desire a son of my lord? did I not say, that thou shouldest not bring me in a fools' paradise? Then he said to Gihezi: gird up thy loins, and take my staff in thine hand and away. If any man meet thee, salute him not. And if any salute thee, answer him not again. And put my staff upon the boy. Notwithstanding the mother of the child said: as sure as the Lord liveth, and as thy soul liveth, I will not leave thee. And then he arose and followed her. Gihezi went before them and put the staff upon the lad. But there was neither voice nor attending. And then he went again against his master and told him saying: it hath not awaked the lad.

And when Eliseus was come to the house: Behold, the lad was dead and laid upon his bed. And he went in and shut the door to the lad and him, and prayed unto the Lord. And he went up and lay upon the lad, and put his mouth on his mouth, and his eyes on his eyes, and the palm of his hands on the palm of his hands, and spread himself upon the lad that the flesh of the child waxed warm. And went again and walked once up and down in the house, and then went up and spread himself upon him. And the lad sneezed seven times and opened his eyes. And he called Gihezi and said: call for this Sunamite. And he called her. And when she was come to him, he said: take thy son. Then she went and fell at his feet and bowed herself to the ground, and took up her son and went out.

[*Complete text*]

Scripture

I do marvel greatly, dearly beloved in Christ, that ever any man should repugn or speak against the scripture to be had in every language, and that of every man. For I thought that no man had been so blind to ask why light should be shewed to them that walk in darkness, where they cannot but stumble, and where to stumble is the danger of eternal damnation: other [or] so despiteful that he would envy any man (I speak not his brother) so necessary a thing: or so Bedlam mad to affirm that good is the natural cause of evil, and darkness to proceed out of light, and that lying should be grounded in truth and verity and not rather clean contrary, that light destroyeth darkness and verity reproveth all manner lying.

Nevertheless, seeing that it hath pleased God to send unto our Englishmen, even to as many as unfeignedly desire it, the scripture in their mother tongue, considering that there be in every place false teachers and blind leaders: that ye should be deceived of no man, I supposed it very necessary to prepare this Pathway into the scripture for you, that ye might walk surely and ever know the true from the false: and, above all, to put you in remembrance of certain points, which are, that ye well understand what these words mean: the Old Testament, the New Testament, the law, the gospel, Moses, Christ, nature, grace, working and believing, deeds and faith, lest we ascribe to the one that which belongeth to the other, and make of Christ Moses: of the gospel, the law: despise grace, and rob faith: and fall from meek learning into idle disputations, brawling and scolding about words.

The Old Testament is a book wherein is written the law of God and the deeds of them which fulfil them and of them also which fulfil them not.

The New Testament is a book wherein are contained the promises of God, and the deeds of them which believe them, or believe them not.

Evangelion (that we call the gospel) is a Greek word and signifieth good, merry, glad and joyful tidings, that maketh a man's heart glad and maketh him sing, dance, and leap for joy: as when David had killed Goliah the giant came glad tidings unto the Jews, that their fearful and cruel enemy was slain and they delivered out of all danger: for gladness whereof they sung, danced, and were joyful. In like manner is the Evangelion of God (which we call gospel, and the New Testament) joyful tidings: and, as some say, a good hearing published by the apostles throughout all the world, of Christ the right David, how that he hath fought with sin, with death, and the devil, and overcome them: whereby all men that were in bondage to sin, wounded with death, overcome of the devil are without their own merits or deservings loosed, justified, restored to life and saved, brought to liberty and reconciled unto the favour of God and set at one with him again: which tidings as many as believe laud, praise and thank God, are glad, sing and dance for joy.

This Evangelion or gospel (that is to say such joyful tidings) is called the New Testament, because that as a man when he shall die, appointeth his goods to be dealt and distributed after his death among them which he nameth to be his heirs, even so Christ before his death commanded and appointed that such Evangelion, gospel, or tidings should be declared throughout all the world, and therewith to give unto all that repent and believe all his goods: that is to say his life wherewith he swallowed and devoured up death, his righteousness, wherewith he banished sin, his salvation, wherewith he overcame eternal damnation. Now can the wretched man (that knoweth himself to be wrapped in sin and in danger to death and hell) hear no more joyous a thing, than such glad and comfortable tidings of Christ, so that he cannot but be glad, and laugh from the low bottom of his heart if he believe that the tidings are true.

To strength such faith withal, God promised this his Evangelion in the Old Testament by the prophets, as Paul saith (Rom. i.) how that he was chosen out to preach God's Evangelion, which he before had promised by the prophets in the Scriptures, that treat of his Son which was born of the seed of David. In Gen. iii. God saith to the serpent, I will put hatred between thee and the woman, between thy seed and her seed, that self seed shall tread thy head under foot. Christ is this woman's seed: he it is that hath trodden under foot the devil's head, that is to say sin, death, hell and all his power. For without this seed can no man avoid sin, death, hell and everlasting damnation.

Again (Gen. xxii.), God promised Abraham, saying, In thy seed shall all the generations of the earth be blessed. Christ is that seed of Abraham, saith St Paul (Gal. iii). He hath blessed all the world through the gospel. For where Christ is not, there remaineth the curse, that fell on Adam as soon as he had sinned, so that they are in bondage under damnation of sin, death and hell. Against this curse blesseth now the gospel all the world inasmuch as it crieth openly unto all that knowledge their sins and repent, saying, Whosoever believeth on the seed of Abraham shall be blessed: that is he shall be delivered from sin, death and hell and shall henceforth continue righteous and saved for ever, as Christ himself saith in the eleventh of John, He that believeth on me, shall never more die.

The law (saith the gospel of John in the first chapter) was given by Moses: but grace and verity by Jesus Christ. The law (whose minister is Moses) was given to bring us unto the knowledge of ourselves, that we might thereby feel and perceive what we are of nature. The law condemneth us and all our deeds and is called of Paul (in 2 Cor. iii.) the ministration of death. For it killeth our consciences and driveth us to desperation, inasmuch as it requireth of us that which is unpossible for our nature to do. It requireth of us the deeds of an whole man. It requireth perfect love, from the low bottom and ground of the heart as well in all things which we suffer, as in the things which we do. But saith John in the same place, grace and verity is given us in Christ: so that, when the law hath passed upon us and condemned us to death (which is his nature to do) then we have in Christ grace, that is to say favour, promises of life, of mercy, of pardon, freely, by the merits of Christ, and in Christ have we verity and truth in that God for his sake fulfilleth all his promises to them that believe. Therefore is the Gospel the ministration of life. Paul calleth it in the fore-rehearsed place of the 2 Cor. iii. the ministration of the Spirit and of righteousness. In the gospel when we believe the promises, we receive the spirit of life, and are justified, in the blood of Christ, from all things whereof the law condemned us. And we receive love unto the law, and power to fulfil it, and grow therein daily. Of Christ it is written, in the fore-rehearsed John i. This is he of whose abundance or fulness all we have received grace for grace or favour for favour. That is to say, For the favour that God hath to his Son Christ, he giveth unto us his favour and good-will and all gifts of his grace, as a father to his sons. As affirmeth Paul, saying, Which loved us in his beloved before the creation of the world. So that Christ bringeth the love of God unto us and not our own holy works. Christ is made Lord over all and is called in scripture God's mercy-stool: whosoever therefore flieth to Christ, can neither hear nor receive of God any other thing save mercy.

In the Old Testament are many promises which are nothing else but the Evangelion or gospel to save those that believed them from the vengeance of the law. And in the New Testament is oft made mention of the law to condemn them which believe not the promises. Moreover, the law and the gospel may never be separate: for the gospel and promises serve but for troubled consciences which are brought to desperation and feel the pains of hell and death under the law and are in captivity and bondage under the law. In all my deeds I must have the law before me, to condemn mine unperfectness. For all that I do (be I never so perfect) is yet damnable sin when it is compared to the law which requireth the ground and bottom of mine heart. I must therefore have always the law in my sight that I may be meek in the spirit and give God all the laud and praise, ascribing to him all righteousness and to myself all unrighteousness and sin. I must also have the promises before mine eyes that I despair not, in which promises I see the mercy, favour and good-will of God upon me in the blood of his Son Christ, which hath made satisfaction for mine unperfectness and fulfilled for me that which I could not do.

Here may ye perceive that two manner of people are sore deceived. First, they which justify themselves with outward deeds in that they abstain outwardly from that which the law forbiddeth and do outwardly that which the law commandeth. They compare themselves to open sinners, and in respect of them justify themselves, condemning the open sinners. They set a vail on Moses' face and see not how the law requireth love from the bottom of the heart, and that love only is the fulfilling of the law. If they did they would not condemn their neighbours. Love hideth the multitude of sins, saith St Peter in his first epistle. For whom I love from the deep bottom and ground of mine heart him condemn I not, neither reckon his sins, but suffer his weakness and infirmity as a mother the weakness of her son until he grow up into a perfect man.

Those also are deceived which without all fear of God give themselves unto all manner vices with full consent and full delectation, having no respect to the law of God (under whose vengeance they are locked up in captivity) but say, God is merciful and Christ died for us, supposing that such dreaming and imagination is that faith which is so greatly commended in holy scripture. Nay, that is not faith but rather a foolish blind opinion springing of their own corrupt nature and is not given them of the Spirit of God, but rather of the spirit of the devil, whose faith now-a-days the popish compare and make equal unto the best trust, confidence and belief that a repenting soul can have in the blood of our Saviour Jesus, unto their own confusion, shame, and uttering what they are within. But true faith is (as saith the apostle Paul) the gift of God, and is given to sinners after the law hath passed upon them and hath brought their consciences unto the brim of desperation and sorrows of hell.

They that have this right faith consent to the law that it is righteous and good, and justify God which made the law, and have delectation in the law (notwithstanding that they cannot fulfil it as they would, for their weakness), and they abhor whatsoever the law forbiddeth though they cannot always avoid it. And their great sorrow is because they cannot fulfil the will of God in the law, and the Spirit that is in them crieth to God night and day for strength and help, with tears (as saith Paul) that cannot be expressed with tongue. Of which things the belief of our popish (or of their) father whom they so magnify for his strong faith hath none experience at all.

The first, that is to say he which justifieth himself with his outward deeds, consenteth not to the law inward, neither hath delectation therein, yea, he would rather that no such law were. So justifieth he not God but hateth him as a tyrant, neither careth he for the promises but will with his own strength be saviour of himself: no wise glorifieth he God though he seem outward to do.

The second, that is to say the sensual person, as a voluptuous swine neither feareth God in his law, neither is thankful to him for his promises and mercy which is set forth in Christ to all them that believe.

The right christian man consenteth to the law that it is righteous and justifieth God in the law, for he affirmeth that God is righteous and just which is author of the law. He believeth the promises of God and justifieth God, judging him true and believing that he will fulfil his promises. With the law he condemneth himself and all his deeds and giveth all the praise to God. He believeth the promises and ascribeth all truth to God: thus everywhere justifieth he God and praiseth God.

By nature through the fall of Adam are we the children of wrath, heirs of the vengeance of God by birth, yea and from our conception. And we have our fellowship with the damned devils, under the power of darkness and rule of Satan, while we are yet in our mother's wombs, and though we shew not forth the fruits of sin as soon as we are born, yet are we full of the natural poison, whereof all sinful deeds spring, and cannot but sin outwards (be we never so young) as soon as we be able to work if occasion be given: for our nature is to do sin as is the nature of a serpent to sting. And as a serpent yet young or yet unbrought forth is full of poison and cannot afterward (when the time is come and occasion given) but bring forth the fruits thereof, and as an adder, a toad or a snake, is hated of man, not for the evil that it hath done but for the poison that is in it and hurt which it cannot but do: so are we hated of God for that natural poison which is conceived and born with us before we do any outward evil. And as the evil which a venomous worm doth maketh it not a serpent, but because it is a venomous worm, doth it evil and poisoneth: and as the fruit maketh not the tree evil, but because it is an evil tree therefore bringeth it forth evil fruit when the season of the fruit is: even so do not our evil deeds make us first evil, though ignorance and blindness, through evil working hardeneth us in evil, and maketh us worse and worse? but because that of nature we are evil therefore we both think and do evil, and are under vengeance under the law, convict to eternal damnation by the law, and are contrary to the will of God in all our will and in all things consent to the will of the fiend.

By grace (that is to say by favour) we are plucked out of Adam the ground of all evil and graffed in Christ, the root of all goodness. In Christ God loved us, his elect and chosen, before the world began and reserved us unto the knowledge of his Son and of his holy gospel: and when the gospel is preached to us openeth our hearts and giveth us grace to believe, and putteth the Spirit of Christ in us: and we know him as our Father most merciful, and consent to the law and love it inwardly in our heart and desire to fulfil it and sorrow because we cannot: which will (sin we of frailty never so much) is sufficient, till more strength be given us: the blood of Christ hath made satisfaction for the rest, the blood of Christ hath obtained all things for us of God. Christ is our satisfaction, Redeemer, Deliverer, Saviour from vengeance and wrath. Observe and mark in Paul's, Peter's and John's epistles and in the gospel what Christ is unto us.

By faith are we saved only in believing the promises. And though faith be never without love and good works, yet is our saving imputed neither to love nor unto good works but unto faith only. For love and works are under the law which requireth perfection and the ground and fountain of the heart and damneth all imperfectness. Now is faith under the promises which damn not, but give pardon, grace, mercy, favour and whatsoever is contained in the promises.

Righteousness is divers[e]: for blind reason imagineth many manner of righteousness. There is the righteousness of works (as I said before) when the heart is away and feeleth not how the law is spiritual and cannot be fulfilled but from the bottom of the heart: as the just ministration of all manner of laws and the observing of them, for a worldly purpose and for our own profit and not of love unto our neighbour without all other respect and moral virtues, wherein philosophers put their felicity and blessedness, which all are nothing in the sight of God in respect of the life to come. There is in like manner the justifying of ceremonies which some imagine their ownselves, some counterfeit, other saying in their blind reason, Such holy persons did thus and thus and they were holy men, therefore if I do so likewise, I shall please God. But they have none answer of God that that pleaseth. The Jews seek righteousness in their ceremonies which God gave unto them not for to justify but to describe and paint Christ unto them: of which Jews testifieth Paul saying, how that they have affection to God but not after knowledge, for they go about to stablish their own justice, and are not obedient to the justice or righteousness that cometh of God, which is the forgiveness of sin in Christ's blood unto all that repent and believe. The cause is verily that except a man cast away his own imagination and reason, he cannot perceive God and understand the virtue and power of the blood of Christ. There is a full righteousness, when the law is fulfilled from the ground of the heart. This had neither Peter nor Paul in this life perfectly unto the uttermost that they could not be perfecter but sighed after it. They were so far forth blessed in Christ that they hungered and thirsted after it. Paul had this thirst: he consented to the law of God that it ought so to be, but he found another lust in his members contrary to the lust and desire of his mind that letted [hindered] him and therefore cried out, saying, O wretched man that I am, who shall deliver me from this body of death? thanks be to God through Jesus Christ. The righteousness that before God is of value, is to believe the promises of God, after the law hath confounded the conscience: as when the temporal law ofttimes condemneth the thief or murderer and bringeth him to execution, so that he seeth nothing before him but present death, and then cometh good tidings, a charter from the king and delivereth him. Likewise, when God's law hath brought the sinner into knowledge of himself and hath confounded his conscience and opened unto him the wrath and vengeance of God, then cometh good tidings. The Evangelion sheweth unto him the promises of God in Christ and how that Christ hath purchased pardon for him, hath satisfied the law for him and appeased the wrath of God. And the poor sinner believeth, laudeth and thanketh God through Christ, and breaketh out into exceeding inward joy and gladness, for that he hath escaped so great wrath, so heavy vengeance, so fearful and so everlasting a death. And he henceforth is an hungred and athirst after more righteousness, that he might fulfil the law, and mourneth continually, commending his weakness unto God in the blood of our Saviour, Christ Jesus.

Here shall ye see compendiously and plainly set out the order and practice of every thing afore rehearsed.

The fall of Adam hath made us heirs of the vengeance and wrath of God and heirs of eternal damnation, and hath brought us into captivity and bondage under the devil And the devil is our lord and our ruler, our head, our governor, our prince, yea and our god. And our will is locked and knit faster unto the will of the devil than could an hundred thousand chains bind a man unto a post. Unto the devil's will consent we with all our hearts, with all our minds, with all our might, power, strength, will and lusts: so that the law and will of the devil is written as well in our hearts as in our members and we run headlong after the devil with full zeal and the whole swing of all the power we have, as a stone cast up into the air cometh down naturally of his own self, with all the violence and swing of his own weight. With what poison, deadly and venomous hate hateth a man his enemy. With how great malice of mind inwardly do we slay and murder. With what violence and rage, yea and with how fervent lust commit we advoutry, fornication and such like uncleanness. With what pleasure and delectation, inwardly, serveth a glutton his belly. With what diligence deceive we. How busily seek we the things of this world. Whatsoever we do, think, or imagine, is abominable in the sight of God. For we can refer nothing unto the honour of

God, neither is his law or will written in our members or in our hearts: neither is there any more power in us to follow the will of God, than in a stone to ascend upward of his own self. And beside that we are as it were asleep in so deep blindness that we can neither see nor feel what misery, thraldom and wretchedness we are in, till Moses come and wake us and publish the law. When we hear the law truly preached, how that we ought to love and honour God with all our strength and might, from the low bottom of the heart, because he hath created us, and both heaven and earth for our sakes, and made us lord thereof, and our neighbours (yea, our enemies) as ourselves, inwardly, from the ground of the heart, because God hath made them after the likeness of his own image, and they are his sons as well as we, and Christ hath bought them with his blood and made them heirs of everlasting life as well as us, and how we ought to do whatsoever God biddeth and abstain from whatsoever God forbiddeth, with all love and meekness, with a fervent and a burning lust from the center of the heart, then beginneth the conscience to rage against the law and against God. No sea be it ever so great a tempest is so unquiet. For it is not possible for a natural man to consent to the law, that it should be good, or that God should be righteous which maketh the law, inasmuch as it is contrary unto his nature and damneth him and all that he can do and neither sheweth him where to fetch help, nor preacheth any mercy, but only setteth man at variance with God (as witnesseth Paul, Rom. iv.) and provoketh him and stirreth him to rail on God and to blaspheme him as a cruel tyrant. For it is not possible for a man, till he be born again, to think that God is righteous to make him of so poison a nature either for his own pleasure or for the sin of another man and to give him a law that is impossible for him to do or to consent to: his wit, reason and will being so fast glued, yea, nailed and chained unto the will of the devil. Neither can any creature loose the bonds, save the blood of Christ only.

This is the captivity and bondage whence Christ delivered us, redeemed and loosed us. His blood, his death, his patience in suffering rebukes and wrongs, his prayers and fastings, his meekness and fulfilling of the uttermost point of the law appeased the wrath of God: brought the favour of God to us again, obtained that God should love us first, and be our Father, and that a merciful Father that will consider our infirmities and weakness and will give us his Spirit again (which was taken away in the fall of Adam) to rule, govern and strength us and to break the bonds of Satan wherein we were so strait bound. When Christ is thuswise preached and the promises rehearsed which are contained in the prophets, in the psalms, and in divers places of the five books of Moses, which preaching is called the Gospel or glad tidings, then the hearts of them which are elect and chosen begin to wax soft and melt at the bounteous mercy of God, and kindness shewed of Christ. For when the Evangelion is preached, the Spirit of God entereth into them which God hath ordained and appointed unto eternal life, and openeth their inward eyes, and worketh such belief in them. When the woful consciences feel and taste how sweet a thing the bitter death of Christ is and how merciful and loving God is through Christ's purchasing and merits, they begin to love again and to consent to the law of God, how that it is good and ought so to be, and that God is righteous which made it, and desire to fulfil the law, even as a sick man desireth to be whole, and are an hungred and thirst after more righteousness and after more strength to fulfil the law more perfectly. And in all that they do, or omit and leave undone, they seek God's honour and his will with meekness, ever condemning the unperfectness of their deeds by the law.

Now Christ standeth us in double stead, and us serveth, two manner wise. First, he is our Redeemer, Deliverer, Reconciler, Mediator, Intercessor, Advocate, Attorney, Solicitor, our Hope, Comfort, Shield, Protection, Defender, Strength, Health, Satisfaction and Salvation. His blood, his death, all that he ever did, is ours. And Christ himself, with all that he is or can do is ours. His blood-shedding and all that he did doth me as good service as though I myself had done it. And God (as great as he is) is mine, with all that he hath, as an husband is his wife's, through Christ and his purchasing.

Secondarily, after that we be overcome with love and kindness and now seek to do the will of God (which is a Christian man's nature) then have we Christ an example to counterfeit, as saith Christ himself in John, I have given you an example. And in another evangelist he saith, He that will be great among you, shall be your servant and minister, as the Son of man came to minister and not to be ministered unto. And Paul saith, Counterfeit Christ. And Peter saith, Christ died for you, and left you an example to follow his steps. Whatsoever therefore faith hath received of God through Christ's blood and deserving, that same must love shed

41

out, every whit and bestow it on our neighbours unto their profit, yea, and that though they be our enemies. By faith we receive of God, and by love we shed out again. And that must we do freely, after the example of Christ without any other respect save our neighbour's wealth [welfare] only, and neither look for reward in the earth nor yet in heaven, for the deserving and merits of our deeds as friars preach, though we know that good deeds are rewarded both in this life and in the life to come. But of pure love must we bestow ourselves, all that we have and all that we are able to do even on our enemies to bring them to God considering nothing but their wealth as Christ did ours. Christ did not his deeds to obtain heaven thereby (that had been a madness): heaven was his already, he was heir thereof, it was his by inheritance: but did them freely for our sakes, considering nothing but our wealth and to bring the favour of God to us again and us to God. And no natural son that is his father's heir doth his father's will because he would be heir, that he is already by birth: his father gave him that ere he was born and is loather that he should go without it, than he himself hath wit to be, but of pure love doth he that he doth. And ask him, Why he doth any thing that he doth? he answereth, My father bade, it is my father's will, it pleaseth my father. Bond-servants work for hire, children for love: for their father, with all he hath, is theirs already. So doth a Christian man freely all that he doth, considereth nothing but the will of God and his neighbour's wealth only. If I live chaste I do it not to obtain heaven thereby, for then should I do wrong to the blood of Christ. Christ's blood hath obtained me that, Christ's merits have made me heir thereof, he is both door and way thitherwards: neither that I look for an higher room in heaven than they shall have which live in wedlock, other [or] than a whore of the stews (if she repent), for that were the pride of Lucifer: but freely to wait on the Evangelion, and to avoid the trouble of the world and occasions that might pluck me therefrom and to serve my brother withal, even as one hand helpeth another or one member another because one feeleth another's grief and the pain of the one is the pain of the other. Whatsoever is done to the least of us (whether it be good or bad) it is done to Christ, and whatsoever is done to my brother (if I be a Christian man) that same is done to me. Neither doth my brother's pain grieve me less than mine own: neither rejoice I less at his wealth than at mine own if I love him as well and as much as myself, as the law commandeth me. If it were not so, how saith

Paul? Let him that rejoiceth, rejoice in the Lord, that is to say Christ which is Lord over all creatures. If my merits obtained me heaven, or a higher place there, then had I wherein I might rejoice besides the Lord.

Here see ye the nature of the law and the nature of the Evangelion: how the law is the key that bindeth and damneth all men and the Evangelion is the key that looseth them again. The law goeth before and the Evangelion followeth. When a preacher preacheth the law he bindeth all consciences, and when he preacheth the gospel he looseth them again. These two salves (I mean the law and the gospel) useth God and his preacher to heal and cure sinners withal. The law driveth out the disease and maketh it appear, and is a sharp salve, and a fretting corosy [corrosive] and killeth the dead flesh and looseth and draweth the sores out by the roots and all corruption. It pulleth from a man the trust and confidence that he hath in himself and in his own works merits, deservings and ceremonies, and robbeth him of all his righteousness, and maketh him poor. It killeth him, sendeth him down to hell and bringeth him to utter desperation and prepareth the way of the Lord, as it is written of John the Baptist. For it is not possible that Christ should come to a man as long as he trusteth in himself or in any worldly thing or hath any righteousness of his own, or riches of holy works. Then cometh the Evangelion, a more gentle pastor which suppleth and suageth the wounds of the conscience and bringeth health. It bringeth the Spirit of God, which looseth the bonds of Satan and coupleth us to God and his will, through strong faith and fervent love, with bonds too strong for the devil, the world or any creature to loose them. And the poor and wretched sinner feeleth so great mercy, love and kindness in God, that he is sure in himself how that it is not possible that God should forsake him, or withdraw his mercy and love from him, and boldly crieth out with Paul, saying, Who shall separate us from the love that God loveth us withal? That is to say, What shall make me believe that God loveth me not? Shall tribulation? anguish? persecution? Shall hunger? nakedness? Shall sword? Nay, I am sure that neither death, nor life, neither angel, neither rule nor power, neither present things nor things to come, neither high nor low, neither any creature, is able to separate us from the love of God, which is in Christ Jesu our Lord. In all such tribulations a Christian man perceiveth that God is his Father and loveth him even as he loved Christ when he shed his blood on the cross. Finally as before, when I was bond to the devil and his will I wrought all manner evil and wickedness, not for hell's sake which is the reward of sin but because I was heir of hell by birth and bondage to the devil, did I evil (for I could none otherwise do, to do sin was my nature) even so now since I am coupled to God by Christ's blood do I well, not for heaven's sake, which is yet the reward of well doing, but because I am heir of heaven by grace and Christ's purchasing, and have the Spirit of God, I do good freely, for so is my nature: as a good tree bringeth forth good fruit and an evil tree evil fruit. By the fruits shall ye know what the tree is. A man's deeds declare what he is within, but make him neither good nor bad, though, after we be created anew by the Spirit and doctrine of Christ, we wax perfecter always with working according to the doctrine and not with blind works of our own imagining. We must be first evil ere we do evil, as a serpent is first poisoned ere he poison. We must be also good ere we do good, as the fire must be first hot, ere it heat another thing. Take an example: As those blind and deaf which are cured in the gospel could not see nor hear till Christ had given them sight and hearing, and those sick could not do the deeds of an whole man till Christ had given them health, so can no man do good in his soul till Christ have loosed him out of the bonds of Satan, and have given him wherewith to do good, yea and first have poured into him that self good thing which he sheddeth forth afterward on other. Whatsoever is our own, is sin. Whatsoever is above that is Christ's gift, purchase, doing and working. He bought it of his Father dearly, with his blood, yea with his most bitter death and gave his life for it. Whatsoever good thing is in us that is given us freely, without our deserving or merits, for Christ's blood's sake. That we desire to follow the will of God it is the gift of Christ's blood. That we now hate the devil's will (whereunto we were so fast locked and could not but love it) is also the gift of Christ's blood, unto whom belongeth the praise and honour of our good deeds, and not unto us.

Our deeds do us three manner of service. First they certify us that we are heirs of everlasting life and that the Spirit of God which is the earnest thereof is in us, in that our hearts consent unto the law of God and we have power in our members to do it though imperfectly. And secondarily we tame the flesh therewith and kill the sin that remaineth yet in us, and wax daily perfecter and perfecter in the Spirit therewith, and keep that the lusts choke not

the word of God that is sown in us, nor quench the ⏐
working of the Spirit and that we lose not the Spirit ag⏐
thirdly we do our duty unto our neighbour therewith, a
their necessity unto our own comfort also and draw all men unto
the honouring and praising of God.

And whosoever excelleth in the gifts of grace let the same think
that they be given him, as much to do his brother service as for his
own self, and as much for the love which God hath to the weak as
unto him unto whom God giveth such gifts. And he that
withdraweth aught that he hath from his neighbour's need
robbeth his neighbour and is a thief. And he that is proud of the
gifts of God and thinketh himself by the reason of them better than
his feeble neighbour and not rather (as the truth is) knowledgeth
himself a servant unto his poor neighbour by the reason of them,
the same hath Lucifer's spirit in him and not Christ's.

These things to know: first the law, how that it is natural right
and equity: that we have but one God to put our hope and trust in
and him to love with all the heart, all the soul and all our might
and power and neither to move heart nor hand but at his
commandment, because he hath first created us of nought and
heaven and earth for our sakes, and afterwards when we had
marred ourself through sin, he forgave us and created us again in
the blood of his beloved Son:

And that we have the name of our one God in fear and
reverence, and that we dishonour it not in swearing thereby
about light trifles or vanity or call it to record for the confirming of wickedness or falsehood or aught that is to the dishonour
of God which is the breaking of his laws or unto the hurt of our
neighbour:

And inasmuch as he is our Lord and God and we his double
possession, by creation and redemption and therefore ought (as I
said) neither to move heart or hand without his commandment, it
is right that we have needful holy days to come together and learn
his will, both the law which he will have us ruled by and also the
promises of mercy which he will have us trust unto, and to give
God thanks together for his mercy and to commit our infirmities
to him through our Saviour Jesus and to reconcile ourselves unto
him and each to other, if aught be between brother and brother
that requireth it. And for this purpose and such like, as to visit the
sick and needy and redress peace and unity, were the holy days
ordained only, and so far forth are they to be kept holy from all

manner works that may be conveniently spared for the time, till this be done and no further but then lawfully to work:

And that it is right that we obey father and mother, master, lord, prince and king and all the ordinances of the world, bodily and ghostly, by which God ruleth us and ministereth freely his benefits unto us all: and that we love them for the benefits that we receive by them and fear them for the power they have over us to punish us, if we trespass the law and good order. So far yet are the worldly powers or rulers to be obeyed only as their commandments repugn not against the commandment of God, and then ho [halt]. Wherefore we must have God's commandment ever in our hearts and by the higher law interpret the inferior, that we obey nothing against the belief of one God, or against the faith, hope and trust that is in him only, or against the love of God whereby we do or leave undone all things for his sake, and that we do nothing for any man's commandment against the reverence of the name of God to make it despised and the less feared and set by, and that we obey nothing to the hinderance of the knowledge of the blessed doctrine of God whose servant the holy day is. Notwithstanding, though the rulers which God hath set over us command us against God or do us open wrong and oppress us with cruel tyranny, yet because they are in God's room we may not avenge ourselves but by the process and order of God's law, and laws of man made by the authority of God's law which is also God's law, ever by an higher power, and remitting the vengeance unto God and in the mean season suffer until the hour be come:

And on the other side to know that a man ought to love his neighbour equally and fully as well as himself, because his neighbour (be he never so simple) is equally created of God and as full redeemed by the blood of our Saviour Jesus Christ. Out of which commandment of love spring these: kill not thy neighbour: defile not his wife: bear no false witness against him: and finally not only do not these things in deed but covet not in thine heart his house, his wife, his man-servant, maid-servant, ox, ass, or whatsoever is his: so that these laws pertaining unto our neighbour are not fulfilled in the sight of God, save with love. He that loveth not his neighbour keepeth not this commandment, Defile not thy neighbour's wife, though he never touch her or never see her or think upon her. For the commandment is, though thy neighbour's wife be never so fair, and thou have never so great opportunity given thee and she consent, or haply provoke thee (as

Potiphar's wife did Joseph) yet see thou love thy neighbour so well that for very love thou cannot find in thine heart to do that wickedness. And even so he that trusteth in any thing save in God only and in his Son Jesus Christ keepeth no commandment at all in the sight of God. For he that hath trust in any creature, whether in heaven or in earth, save in God and his Son Jesus, can see no cause to love God with all his heart &c. neither to abstain from dishonouring his name, nor to keep the holy day for the love of his doctrine, nor to obey lovingly the rulers of this world, nor any cause to love his neighbour as himself and to abstain from hurting him where he may get profit by him and save himself harmless. And in like wise, against this law, Love thy neighbour as thyself, I may obey no worldly power to do aught at any man's commandment unto the hurt of my neighbour that hath not deserved it though he be a Turk:

And to know how contrary this law is unto our nature and how it is damnation not to have this law written in our hearts though we never commit the deeds, and how there is no other means to be saved from this damnation, than through repentance toward the law and faith in Christ's blood, which are the very inward baptism of our souls, and the washing and the dipping of our bodies in the water is the outward sign. The plunging of the body under the water signifieth that we repent and profess to fight against sin and lusts and to kill them every day more and more with the help of God and our diligence in following the doctrine of Christ and the leading of his Spirit, and that we believe to be washed from our natural damnation in which we are born and from all the wrath of the law and from all the infirmities and weaknesses that remain in us after we have given our consent unto the law and yielded ourself to be scholars thereof, and from all the imperfectness of all our deeds done with cold love, and from all actual sin which shall chance on us while we enforce the contrary and ever fight there against and hope to sin no more. And thus repentance and faith begin at our baptism and first professing the laws of God, and continue unto our lives' end and grow as we grow in the Spirit: for the perfecter we be the greater is our repentance and the stronger our faith. And thus, as the Spirit and doctrine on God's part, and repentance and faith on our part, beget us anew in Christ, even so they make us grow and wax perfect and save us unto the end, and never leave us until all sin be put off and we clean purified and full formed and fashioned after the similitude and likeness of the perfectness of our Saviour Jesus whose gift all is:

And finally to know that whatsoever good thing is in us, that same is the gift of grace and therefore not of deserving, though many things be given of God through our diligence in working his laws and chastising our bodies and in praying for them, and believing his promises, which else should not be given us: yet our working deserveth not the gifts, no more than the diligence of a merchant in seeking a good ship bringeth the goods safe to land though such diligence doth now and then help thereto: but when we believe in God and then do all that is in our might and not tempt him, then is God true to abide by his promise and to help us and perform alone when our strength is past:

These things I say to know is to have all the scripture unlocked and opened before thee, so that if thou wilt go in and read, thou canst not but understand. And in these things to be ignorant is to have all the scripture locked up, so that the more thou readest it, the blinder thou art and the more contrariety thou findest in it and the more tangled art thou therein and canst nowhere through: for if thou had a gloss in one place, in another it will not serve. And therefore because we be never taught the profession of our baptism we remain always unlearned, as well the spiritualty for all their great clergy and high schools (as we say) as the lay people. And now, because the lay and unlearned people are taught these first principles of our profession, therefore they read the scripture and understand and delight therein. And our great pillars of holy church, which have nailed a veil of false glosses on Moses's face to corrupt the true understanding of his law cannot come in. And therefore they bark and say the scripture maketh heretics, and it is not possible for them to understand it in the English, because they themselves do not in Latin. And of pure malice that they cannot have their will, they slay their brethren for their faith they have in our Saviour and therewith utter their bloody wolfish tyranny and what they be within and whose disciples. Herewith reader be committed unto the grace of our Saviour Jesus, unto whom and God our Father through him be praise for ever and for ever. Amen.

From *The Parable of the Wicked Mammon*, 1528

There was a certain rich man which had a steward, that was accused unto him, that he had wasted his goods: and he called him, and said unto him: How is it that I hear this of thee? Give account of thy stewardship, for thou mayest be no longer my steward. The steward said within himself, What shall I do, for my master will take away from me my stewardship? I cannot dig, and to beg I am ashamed. I wot what to do, that when I am put out of my stewardship they may receive me into their houses. Then called he all his master's debtors and said unto the first, How much owest thou unto my master? And he said, An hundred tons of oil. And he said to him, Take thy bill and sit down quickly and write fifty. Then said he to another, What owest thou? And he said, An hundred quarters of wheat. He said to him, Take thy bill and write fourscore. And the lord commended the unjust steward, because he had done wisely. For the children of this world are in their kind wiser than the children of light. And I say also unto you, Make you friends of the wicked mammon [riches], that when ye shall have need, they may receive you into everlasting habitations (Luke xvi).

Forasmuch as with this and divers such other texts, many have enforced to draw the people from the true faith and from putting their trust in the truth of God's promises and in the merits and deserving of his Christ our Lord, and have also brought it to pass, (for many false prophets shall arise and deceive many, and much wickedness must also be, saith Christ: and Paul saith, Evil men and deceivers shall prevail in evil, while they deceive, and are deceived themselves) and have taught them to put their trust in their own merits and brought them in belief that they shall be justified in the sight of God by the goodness of their own works, and have corrupted the pure word of God, to confirm their Aristotle withal, (for though that the philosophers and worldly wise men were enemies above all enemies to the gospel of God, and though the worldly wisdom cannot comprehend the wisdom of God, as thou mayest see 1 Cor. i. and ii., and though worldly righteousness cannot be obedient unto the righteousness of God, yet whatsoever they read in Aristotle that must be first true, and to maintain that they rend and tear the scriptures with their distinctions and expound them violently, contrary to the meaning of the text, and to the circumstances that go before and after, and to a thousand clear and evident texts:) wherefore I have taken in hand to expound this gospel and certain other places of the New Testament, and (as far forth as God shall lend me grace) to bring the scripture unto the right sense and to dig again the wells of Abraham and to purge and cleanse them of the earth of worldly wisdom, wherewith these Philistines have stopped them. Which grace grant me God for the love that he hath unto his Son Jesus our Lord unto the glory of his name. Amen.

That faith only before all works and without all merits but Christ's only justifieth and setteth us at peace with God is proved by Paul in the first chapter to the Romans. I am not ashamed (saith he) of the gospel, that is to say of the glad tidings and promises which God hath made and sworn to us in Christ: for it (that is to say the gospel) is the power of God unto salvation to all that believe. And it followeth in the foresaid chapter, the just or righteous must live by faith.

For in the faith which we have in Christ and in God's promises find we mercy, life, favour and peace. In the law we find death, damnation and wrath, moreover the curse and vengeance of God upon us. And it (that is to say the law) is called of Paul the ministration of death and damnation. In the law we are proved to be the enemies of God and that we hate him. For how can we be at peace with God and love him, seeing we are conceived and born under the power of the devil and are his possession and kingdom, his captives and bondmen and led at his will, and he holdeth our hearts, so that it is impossible for us to consent to the will of God, much more is it impossible for a man to fulfil the law of his own strength and power, seeing that we are by birth and of nature the heirs of eternal damnation, as saith Paul, Eph. ii.? We (saith he) are by nature the children of wrath, which thing the law doth but utter only, and helpeth us not yea, requireth impossible things of us. The law when it commandeth that thou shalt not lust giveth thee not power so to do but damneth thee because thou canst not so do.

If thou wilt therefore be at peace with God and love him, thou must turn to the promises of God and to the gospel which is called of Paul, in the place before rehearsed to the Corinthians, the ministration of righteousness and of the Spirit. For faith bringeth pardon and forgiveness freely purchased by Christ's blood and bringeth also the Spirit: the Spirit looseth the bonds of the devil and setteth us at liberty. For where the Spirit of the Lord is, there is liberty, saith Paul in the same place to the Corinthians: that is to say, there the heart is free and hath power to love the will of God, and there the heart mourneth that he cannot love enough. Now is that consent of the heart unto the law of God eternal life, yea though there be no power yet in the members to fulfil it. Let every man therefore (according to Paul's counsel in the sixth chapter to the Ephesians) arm himself with the armour of God, that is to understand with God's promises. And above all things (saith he) take unto you the shield of faith, wherewith ye may be able to quench the fiery darts of the wicked, that ye may be able to resist in the evil day of temptation, and namely at the hour of death.

See therefore thou have God's promises in thine heart and that thou believe them without wavering: and when temptation ariseth, and the devil layeth the law and thy deeds against thee, answer him with the promises, and turn to God and confess thyself to him and say it is even so, or else how could he be merciful? But remember that he is the God of mercy and of truth and cannot but fulfil his promises. Also remember that his Son's blood is stronger than all the sins and wickedness of the whole world, and therewith quiet thyself and hereunto commit thyself and bless thyself in all temptation (namely at the hour of death) with that holy candle. Or else perishest thou though thou hast a thousand holy candles about thee, a hundred ton of holy water, a ship-full of pardons, a cloth-sack full of friars' coats and all the ceremonies in the world and all the good works, deservings and merits of all the men in the world, be they, or were they, never so holy. God's word only lasteth for ever, and that which he hath sworn doth abide when all other things perish. So long as thou findest any consent in thine heart unto the law of God that it is righteous and good and also displeasure that thou canst not fulfil it despair not, neither doubt but that God's Spirit is in thee and that thou art chosen for Christ's sake to the inheritance of eternal life.

From *The Obedience of a Christian Man*, 1528

William Tyndale otherwise called William Hychins unto the reader

Grace, peace and increase of knowledge in our Lord Jesus Christ be with the reader and with all that call on the name of the Lord unfeignedly and with a pure conscience, Amen.

Let it not make thee despair neither yet discourage thee O reader, that it is forbidden thee in pain of life and goods or that it is made breaking of the King's peace or treason unto His Highness to read the word of thy soul's health. But much rather be bold in the Lord and comfort thy soul. Forasmuch as thou art pure and hast an evident token through such persecution that it is the true word of God. Which word is ever hated of the world, neither was ever without persecution (as thou seest in all the stories of the Bible both of the New Testament and also of the Old) neither can be, no more than the sun can be without his light. And forasmuch as contrarywise thou art sure that the Pope's doctrine is not of God which (as thou seest) is so agreeable unto the world, and is so received of the world or which rather so receiveth the world and the pleasures of the world, and seeketh nothing but the possessions of the world, and authority in the world, and to bear a rule in the world, and persecuteth the word of God, and with all wiliness driveth the people from it, and with false and sophistical reasons maketh them afeared of it: yea curseth them and excommunicateth them, and bringeth them in belief that they be damned, if they look on it, and that it is but doctrine to deceive men, and moveth the blind powers of the world to slay with fire, water, and sword all that cleave unto it. For the world loveth that which is his, and hateth that which is chosen out of the world to serve God in the spirit. As Christ saith to his disciples (John 15) if ye were of the world, the world would love his own. But I have chosen you out of the world and therefore the world hateth you.

Another comfort hast thou, that as the weak powers of the world defend the doctrine of the world so the mighty power of God defendeth the doctrine of God. Which thing thou shalt evidently perceive, if thou call to mind the wonderful deeds which God hath ever wrought for his word in extreme necessity since the world began beyond all man's reason. Which are written as saith Paul (Romans 15) for our learning (and not for our deceiving) that we through patience, and comfort of the scripture might have hope. The nature of God's word is to fight against hypocrites. It began at Abel and hath ever since continued and shall, I doubt not, until the last day. And the hypocrites have always the world on their sides, as thou seest in time of Christ. They had the elders, that is to wit the rulers of the Jews, on their side. They had Pilate and the emperor's power on their side. They had Herod also on their side. Moreover they brought all their worldly wisdom to pass and all that they could think or imagine to serve for their purpose. First to fear the people withal, they excommunicated all that believed in him, and put them out of the temple, as thou seest (John 9). Secondly they found the means to have him condemned by the emperor's power and made it treason to Caesar to believe in him. Thirdly they obtained to have him hanged as a thief or a murderer, which after their belly wisdom was a cause above all causes, that no man should believe in him. For the Jews take it for a sure token of everlasting damnation if a man be hanged. For it is written in their law (Deuteronomy 21) cursed is whosoever hangeth on a tree. Moses also in the same place commandeth, if any man be hanged, to take him down the same day and bury him, for fear of polluting or defiling the country, that is, lest they should bring the wrath and curse of God upon them. And therefore the wicked Jews themselves, which with so venomous hate persecuted the doctrine of Christ and did all the shame that they could do unto him (though they would fain have had Christ to hang stiff on the cross and there to rot, as he should have done by the emperor's law), yet for fear of defiling their Sabbath and of bringing the wrath and curse of God upon them begged of Pilate to take him down (John 19), which was against themselves. Finally when they had done all they could and that they thought sufficient, and when Christ was in the heart of the earth and so many bills and poleaxes about him, to keep him down, and when it was past man's help: then holp God. When man could not bring him again, God's truth fetched him again. The oath that God had sworn to Abraham, to David and to other holy fathers and prophets raised him up again, to bless and to save all that believe in him. Thus became the wisdom of the hypocrites foolishness. Lo this was written for thy learning and comfort.

How wonderfully were the children of Israel locked in Egypt? In what tribulation, cumbrance and adversity were they in? The land also that was promised them, was far off and full of great cities walled with high walls up to the sky and inhabited with great giants. Yet God's truth brought them out of Egypt and planted them in the land of the giants. This was also written for our learning, for there is no power against God's neither any wisdom against God's wisdom: he is stronger and wiser than all his enemies. What holp it Pharaoh to drown the men children? So little, I fear not, shall it at the last help the Pope and his bishops to burn our men children which manfully confess that Jesus is the Lord and that there is no other name given unto men to be saved by, as Peter testifeth (Acts in the fourth chapter). Who dried up the Red Sea? Who slew Goliath? Who did all those wonderful deeds which thou readest in the Bible? Who delivered the Israelites evermore from thraldom and bondage, as soon as they repented and turned to God? Faith verily and God's truth and the trust in the promises which he had made. Read the eleventh chapter to the Hebrews for thy consolation.

*

The sermons which thou readest in the Acts of the Apostles and all that the apostles preached were no doubt preached in the mother tongue. Why then might they not be written in the mother tongue? As if one of us preach a good sermon why may it not be written? Saint Jerome also translated the Bible into his mother tongue. Why may not we also? They will say it cannot be translated into our tongue it is so rude. It is not so rude as they are false liars. For the Greek tongue agreeth more with the English than with the Latin. And the properties of the Hebrew tongue agreeth a thousand times more with the English than with the Latin. The manner of speaking is both one, so that in a thousand places thou needest not but to translate it into the English word for word when thou must seek a compass in the Latin, and yet shalt have much work to translate it well favouredly, so that it have the same grace and sweetness, sense and pure understanding with it in the Latin, as it hath in the Hebrew. A thousand parts better may it be translated into the English than into the Latin. Yea and except my memory fail me and that I have forgotten what I read when I was a child thou shalt find in the English chronicle how the king

Athelstan caused the Holy Scripture to be translated into the tongue that then was in England and how the prelates exhorted him thereunto.

*

God (which worketh all in all things) for a secret judgment and purpose and for his godly pleasure, provided an hour that thy father and mother should come together, to make thee through them. He was present with thee in thy mother's womb and fashioned thee and breathed life into thee, and for the great love he had unto thee, provided milk in thy mother's breasts for thee against thou were born: moved also thy father and mother and all other to love thee, to pity thee and to care for thee.

And as he made thee through them, so hath he cast thee under the power and authority of them, to obey and serve them in his stead saying: honour thy father and mother (Exodus 20). Which is not to be understood in bowing the knee and putting off the cap only, but that thou love them with all thine heart and fear and dread them and wait on their commandments and seek their worship, pleasure, will and profit in all things, and give thy life for them counting them worthy of all honour, remembering that thou art their good and possession, and that thou owest unto them thine own self and all that thou art able, yea and more than thou art able to do.

Understand also that whatsoever thou doest unto them (be it good or bad) thou doest unto God. When thou pleasest them thou pleasest God: when thou displeasest them thou displeasest God: when they are angry with thee, God is angry with thee, neither is it possible for thee to come unto the favour of God again (no though all the angels of heaven pray for thee) until thou have submitted thyself unto thy father and mother again.

*

To preach God's word is too much for half a man. And to minister a temporal kingdom is too much for half a man also. Either other requireth an whole man. One therefore cannot well do both. He that avengeth himself on every trifle is not meet to preach the patience of Christ, how that a man ought to forgive and to suffer all things. He that is overwhelmed with all manner riches and doth but seek more daily, is not meet to preach poverty. He that will obey no man is not meet to preach how we ought to obey all men. Peter saith (Acts 6), It is not meet that we should leave the word of God and serve at the tables. Paul saith in the ninth chapter of the first Corinthians, God sent me but to preach. A terrible saying verily for popes, cardinals, and bishops. If he had said woe be to me if I fight not and move princes unto war. Or if I increase not Saint Peter's patrimony (as they call it) it had been a more easy saying for them.

*

First by the authority of the gospel, they that preach the word of God in every parish and other necessary ministers have right to challenge an honest living like unto one of the brethren, and therewith ought to be content. Bishops and priests that preach not or that preach ought save God's word, are none of Christ's nor of his anointing: but servants of the beast whose mark they bear, whose word they preach, whose law they maintain clean against God's law, and with their false sophistry give him greater power than God ever gave to his son Christ.

But they as unsatiable beasts not unmindful why they were shaven and shorn, because they will stand at no man's grace or be in any man's danger, have gotten into their own hands, first the tithe or tenth of all the realm: Then I suppose within a little or all together the third foot of all the temporal lands.

Mark well how many parsonages or vicarages are there in the realm which at the least have a ploughland apiece. Then note the lands of bishops, abbots, priors, nuns, knights of Saint John's, cathedral churches, colleges, chantries and freechapels. For though the house fall in decay and the ordinance of the founder be lost, yet will not they lose the lands. What cometh once in, may never more out. They make a freechapel of it, so that he which enjoyeth it shall do nought therefore. Besides all this, how many chaplains do gentlemen find at their own cost in their houses? How many sing for souls by testaments? Then the proving of testaments, the pressing of goods (the bishop of Canterbury's prerogative). Is that not much through the realm in a year? Four offering days and privy tithes? There is no servant, but that he shall pay somewhat of his wages. None shall receive the body of Christ at Easter, be he never so poor a beggar or never so young a lad or maid, but they must pay somewhat for it. Then mortuaries for forgotten tithes (as they say). And yet what person or vicar is there that will forget to have a pigeon house to peck up somewhat both at sowing time and at harvest when corn is ripe? They will forget nothing. No man shall die in their debt, or if any man do, he shall pay it when he is dead. They will lose nothing. Why? It is God's, it is not theirs. It is Saint Cuthbert's rents, Saint Alban's lands, Saint Edmund's right, Saint Peter's patrimony say they, and none of ours. Item if a man die in another man's parish, besides that he must pay at home a mortuary for forgotten tithes, he must there pay also the best that he there hath. Whether it be an horse of twenty pound or how good soever he be, either a chain of gold of an hundred mark or five hundred pound, if it so chance. It is much verily for so little pain-taking in confessions and in ministering the sacraments. Then beadrolls. Item chrisom, churchings, banns, weddings, offering at weddings, offering at buryings, offering to images, offering of wax and lights which come to their vantage, besides the superstitious waste of wax in torches and tapers throughout the land. Then brotherhoods and pardoners. What get they also by confessions? Yea and many enjoin penance to give a certain, for to have so many masses said, and desire to provide a chaplain and themselves. Soul masses, diriges, month minds, years' minds, All Souls day and trentals. The mother church and the high altar must have somewhat in every testament. Offerings at priests' first masses. Item no man is professed, of whatsoever religion it be, but he must bring somewhat. The hallowing or rather conjuring of churches, chapels, altars, superaltars, chalice vestments and bells. Then book, bell, candlestick, organs, chalice, vestments, copes, altar cloths, surplices: towels, basins, ewers, ship, censer and all manner ornaments must be found them freely, they will not give a mite thereunto. Last of all what swarms of begging friars are there? The parson sheareth, the vicar shaveth, the parish priest polleth, the friar scrapeth and the pardoner pareth. We lack but a butcher to pull off the skin.

*

The Emperor and kings are nothing nowadays but even hangmen unto the Pope and bishops, to kill whosoever they condemn, without any more ado, as Pilate was unto the scribes and Pharisees and the high bishops, to hang Christ. For as those prelates answered Pilate (when he asked what he had done) if he were not an evil doer we would not have brought him unto thee. As who should say, we are too holy to do anything amiss, thou mayest believe us well enough: yea and his blood on our heads, said they, kill him hardly, we will bear the charge, our souls for thine: we have also a law by which he ought to die, for he calleth himself God's son. Even so say our prelates, he ought to die by our laws, he speaketh against the church. And your grace is sworn to defend the liberties and ordinances of the church and to maintain our most holy father's authority: our souls for yours, ye shall do a meritorious deed therein. Nevertheless as Pilate escaped not the judgment of God, even so is it to be feared lest our temporal powers shall not. Wherefore be learned ye that judge the earth lest the Lord be angry with you and ye perish from the right way.

Who slew the prophets? Who slew Christ? Who slew his Apostles? Who the martyrs and all the righteous that ever were slain? The kings and the temporal sword at the request of the false prophets. They deserved such murder to do and to have their part with the hypocrites because they would not be learned and see the truth themselves. Wherefore suffered the prophets? Because they rebuked the hypocrites which beguiled the world and namely princes and rulers and taught them to put their trust in things of vanity and not in God's word. And taught them to do such deeds of mercy as were profitable unto no man but unto the false prophets themselves only, making merchandise of God's word. Wherefore slew they Christ? Even for rebuking the hypocrites: because he said, woe be to you scribes and Pharisees, hypocrites, for ye shut up the kingdom of heaven before men (Matthew 23) that is, as it is written (Luke 11), Ye have taken away the key of knowledge. The law of God which is the key wherewith men bind, and the promises which are the keys wherewith men loose, have our hypocrites also taken away. They will suffer no man to know God's word but burn it and make heresy of it: yea and because the people begin to smell their falsehood they make it treason to the king and breaking of the king's peace to have so much as their *Pater Noster* in English. And instead of God's law, they bind with their own law. And instead of God's promises they loose and justify with pardons and ceremonies which they themselves have imagined for their own profit. They preach it were better for thee to eat flesh on Good Friday than to hate thy neighbour: but let any man eat flesh but on a Saturday or break any other tradition of theirs, and he shall be bound and not loosed, till he have paid the uttermost farthing, other with shame most vile or death most cruel, but hate thy neighbour as much as thou wilt and thou shalt have no rebuke of them, yea rob him, murder him, and then come to them and welcome. They have a sanctuary for thee, to save thee, yea and a neckverse, if thou canst but read a little Latin though it be never so sorely, so that thou be ready to receive the beast's mark. They care for no understanding, it is enough, if thou canst roll up a pair of matins or an evensong and mumble a few ceremonies. And because they be rebuked, this they rage. Be learned therefore ye that judge the world lest God be angry with you and ye perish from the right way.

*

Woe be to you scribes and Pharisees, hypocrites. For ye make clean the utter side of the cup and of the platter, but within they are full of bribery and excess saith Christ (Matthew 23). Is that which our hypocrites eat and drink and all their riotous excess any other thing save robbery and that which they have falsely gotten with their lying doctrine? Be learned therefore ye that judge the world and compel them to make retribution again.

Ye blind guides saith Christ, ye strain out a gnat and swallow a camel (Matthew 23). Do not our blind guides also stumble at a straw and leap over a block, making narrow consciences at trifles, and at matters of weight none at all. If any of them happen to swallow his spittle or any of the water wherewith he washeth his mouth, ere he go to mass, or touch the sacrament with his nose or if the ass forget to breathe on him or happen to handle it with any of his fingers which are not anointed, or say *Alleluia* instead of *Laus tibi domine* or *Ite missa est* instead of *Benedicamus domino* or pour too much wine in the chalice, or read the gospel without light, or make not his crosses aright, how trembleth he? How feareth he? What an horrible sin is committed? I cry God mercy, saith he, and you my ghostly father. But to hold an whore or another man's wife, to buy a benefice, or set one realm at variance with another and to cause twenty thousand men to die on a day is but a trifle and a pastime with them.

*

Nevertheless the truth is, that we are all equally beloved in Christ, and God hath sworn to all indifferently. According therefore as every man believeth God's promises, longeth for them and is diligent to pray unto God to fulfil them so is his prayer heard, and as good is the prayer of a cobbler, as of a cardinal, and of a butcher, as of a bishop, and the blessing of a baker that knoweth the truth, is as good as the blessing of our most holy father the Pope. And by blessing understand not the wagging of the Pope's or the bishop's hand over thine head, but prayer as when we say God make thee a good man, Christ put his Spirit in thee or give thee grace and power to walk in the truth and to follow his commandments etc. As Rebecca's friends blessed her when she departed (Genesis 24), saying, thou art our sister: grow unto thousand thousands and thy seed possess the gates of their enemies. And as Isaac blessed Jacob (Genesis 27) saying, God give thee of the dew of heaven and of the fatness of the earth abundance of corn, wine and oil etc. And (Genesis 28), Almighty God bless thee and make thee grow, and multiply thee, that thou mayest be a great multitude of people and give to thee and to thy seed after thee the blessings of Abraham, that thou mayest possess the land wherein thou art a stranger which he promised to thy grandfather and such like.

*

But contrarywise unto monks, friars, and to the other of our holy spirituality the belly is all in all and cause of all love. Offer thereto, so art thou father, mother, sister, and brother unto them. Offerest thou not, so know they thee not, thou art neither father, mother, sister, brother nor any kin at all to them. She is a sister of ours, he is a brother of ours, say they: he is verily a good man, for he doeth much for our religion. She is a mother to our convent: we be greatly bound to pray for them. And as for such and such (say they) we know not whether they be good or bad or whether they be fish or flesh, for they do nought for us: we be more bound to pray for our benefactors (say they) and for them that give us, than for them that give us not. For them that give little are they little bound and them they love little and for them that give much are they much bound and them they love much. And for them that give nought are they nought bound and them they love not at all. And as they love thee when thou givest: so hate they thee when thou takest away from them, and run all under a stole and curse thee as black as pitch. So is cloister love belly love, cloister prayer belly prayer, and cloister brotherhood belly brotherhood. Moreover love that springeth of Christ seeketh not her own self (1 Corinthians 13) but forgetteth herself and bestoweth her upon her neighbour's profit as Christ sought our profit and not his own. He sought not the favour of God for himself, but for us: yea he took the wrath and vengeance of God from us unto himself and bare it on his own back to bring us unto favour. Likewise doth a Christian man give to his brethren and robbeth them not as friars and monks do: but as Paul commandeth (Ephesians 4) laboureth with his hands some good work to have wherewith to help the needy. They give not but receive only. They labour not but live idly of the sweat of the poor. There is none so poor a widow, though she have not to find herself and her children nor any money to give: yet shall the friar snatch a cheese or somewhat. They preach, sayest thou, and labour in the word. First I say they are not called and therefore ought not: for it is the curate's office. The curate cannot, sayest thou. What doeth the thief there then? Secondarily a true preacher preacheth Christ's testament only and maketh Christ the cause and reward of all our deeds and teacheth every man to bear his cross willingly for Christ's sake. But these are enemies unto the cross of Christ and preach their belly which is their God (Ephesians 3) and they think that lucre is the serving of God (1 Timothy 6). That is, they think them Christian only which offer unto their bellies, which when thou has filled then spew they out prayers for thee, to be thy reward, and yet wot not what prayer meaneth. Prayer is the longing for God's promises, which promises as they preach them not, so long they not for them nor wish them unto any man. Their longing is to fill their paunch whom they serve and not Christ, and through sweet preaching and flattering words deceive the hearts of the simple and unlearned (Romans 16).

The four senses of the scripture

They divide the scripture into four senses, the literal, tropological, allegorical, anagogical. The literal sense is becoming nothing at all. For the Pope hath taken it clean away and hath made it his possession. He hath partly locked it up with the false and counterfeited keys of his traditions, ceremonies and feigned lies. And partly driveth men from it with violence of sword. For no man dare abide by the literal sense of the text, but under a protestation, if it shall please the Pope. The tropological sense pertaineth to good manners (say they) and teacheth what we ought to do. The allegory is appropriate to faith, and the anagogical to hope and things above. Tropological and anagogical are terms of their own feigning and altogether unnecessary. For they are but allegories both two of them and this word allegory comprehendeth them both and is enough. For chopological is but an allegory of manners and anagogical an allegory of hope. And allegory is as much to say as strange speaking or borrowed speech. As when we say of a wanton child, this sheep hath maggots in his tail, he must be anointed with birchen salve which speech I borrow of the shepherds.

Thou shalt understand therefore that the scripture hath but one sense which is the literal sense. And that literal sense is the root and ground of all, and the anchor that never faileth whereunto if thou cleave thou canst never err or go out of the way. And if thou leave the literal sense thou canst not but go out of the way. Neverthelater the scripture useth proverbs, similitudes, riddles or allegories as all other speeches do, but that which the proverb, similitude, riddle or allegory signifieth is ever the literal sense which thou must seek out diligently. As in the English we borrow words and sentences of one thing and apply them unto another and give them new significations. We say let the sea swell and rise as high as he will yet hath God appointed how far he shall go: meaning that the tyrants shall not do what they would, but that only which God hath appointed them to do. Look ere thou leap, whose literal sense is, do nothing suddenly or without advisement. Cut not the bough that thou standest upon, whose literal sense is oppress not the commons and is borrowed of hewers. When a thing speedeth not well, we borrow speech and say, the bishop hath blessed it, because that nothing speedeth well that they meddle withal. If the porridge be burned too, or the meat over-roasted, we say, the bishop hath put his foot in the pot or the bishop hath played the cook, because the bishops burn whom they lust and whosoever displeaseth them. He is a pontifical fellow, that is, proud and stately. He is popish, that is, superstitious and faithless. It is a pastime for a prelate. It is a pleasure for a Pope. He would be free and yet will not have his head shaven. He would that no man should smite him and yet hath not the Pope's mark. And of him that is betrayed and wotteth not how, we say, he hath been at shrift. She is master parson's sister's daughter. He is the bishop's sister's son, he hath a cardinal to his uncle, she is a spiritual whore, it is the gentlewoman of the parsonage, he gave me a *Kyrie eleison.* And of her that answereth her husband six words for one we say, she is a sister of the Charterhouse, as who should say, she thinketh that she is not bound to keep silence, their silence shall be a satisfaction to her. And of him that will not be saved by Christ's merits, but by the works of his own imagination we say it is a holyworkman. Thus borrow we and feign new speech in every tongue. All fables, prophecies and riddles are allegories and Aesop's fables and Merlin's prophecies and the interpretation of them are the literal sense.

So in like manner the scripture borroweth words and sentences of all manner things and maketh proverbs and similitudes or allegories. As Christ saith (Luke 4), Physician heal thyself. Whose interpretation is do that at home which thou doest in strange places, and that is the literal sense. So when I say Christ is a lamb, I mean not a lamb that beareth wool, but a meek and a patient lamb which is beaten for other men's faults. Christ is a vine, not that beareth grapes: but out of whose root the branches that believe suck the spirit of life and mercy and grace and power to be the sons of God and to do his will. The similitudes of the gospel are allegories borrowed of worldly matter to express spiritual things. The Apocalypse or Revelations of John are allegories whose literal sense is hard to find in many places.

*

I was once at the creating of doctors of divinity, where the opponent brought the same reason to prove that the widow had more merit than the virgin, because she had greater pains forasmuch as she had once proved the pleasures of matrimony. *Ego nego domine doctor* said the respondent. For though the virgin have not proved, yet she imagineth that the pleasure is greater than it is indeed and therefore is more moved and hath greater temptation and greater pain. Are not these disputers they that Paul speaketh of in the sixth chapter of the first epistle to Timothy? That they are not content with the wholesome words of our Lord Jesus

Christ, and doctrine of godliness? And therefore know nothing: but waste their brains about questions and strife of words, whereof spring envy, strife and railing of men with corrupt minds destitute of the truth.

From *An Exposition upon the First Epistle of St John*, 1531

[Part of a long commentary on the opening of chapter two]

But after what manner doth Christ pray for us? Verily Christ in the days of his mortal flesh suffered and prayed for all that shall be saved and obtained and was heard and had his petitions granted. And he made satisfaction and purged and purchased forgiveness, even then, for all the sin that ever shall be forgiven. And his praying for us and being a mediator now is that the remembrance of all that he did for us is present in the sight of God the Father, as fresh as the hour he did them, yea, the same hour is yet present, and not past in the sight of God. And Christ is now a king and reigneth, and hath received power of all that he prayed for to do it himself, and that whensoever the elect call for aught in his name he sendeth help even of the power which he hath received, yea, ere they ask, he sendeth his Spirit into their hearts to move them to ask: so that it is his gift that we desire aught in his name. And in all that we do or think well he preventeth us with his grace: yea, he careth for us ere we care for ourselves and when we be yet evil he sendeth to call us, and draweth us with such power that our hearts cannot but consent and come and the angels stand by and behold the testament of the elect, how we shall be received into their fellowship, and see all the grace that Christ shall pour out upon us. And they rejoice and praise God for his infinite mercy, and are glad and long for us, and of very love are ready against all hours when we shall call for help in Christ's name, to come and help. And Christ sendeth them when we call in his name, and ere we call even while we be yet evil and haply persecute the truth of ignorance as Paul did, the angels wait upon us to keep that the devils slay us not before the time of our calling be come.

Now if an angel should appear unto thee, what wouldest thou say unto him? If thou prayedst him to help, he would answer: I do. Christ hath sent me to help thee, and believe that the angels be ever about thee to help. If thou desiredst him to pray for thee, to obtain this or that, he would say: Christ hath prayed, and his prayer is heard for whatsoever thou askest in his name, and would shew thee all that God would do to thee and what he would also have thee to do: and if thou believest so, then wert thou safe. If thou desiredst him to save thee with his merits, he would answer that he had no merits, but that Christ only is Lord of all merits, nor salvation, but that Christ is Lord of salvation. Wilt thou therefore be saved by merits? would the angel say, then pray to God in Christ's name, and thou shalt be saved by the merits of him, and have me, or some other thy servant immediately to help thee unto the uttermost of our power and to keep thee and bring thee unto the reward of his merits. If thou wouldest promise him to worship him with image-service, that is, to stick up a candle before his image or such an image as he appeared to thee in, he would answer that he were a spirit and delighted in no candle-light, but would bid thee give a candle to thy neighbour that lacketh, if thou hadst too many. And so would he answer thee, if thou wouldest put money in a box for him, or clothe his image in cloth of gold, or put golden shoes upon his image's feet. If thou saidst that thou wouldest build a chapel in his name, he would answer that he dwelt in no house made with stones, but would bid thee go to the churches that are made already and learn of the preachers there how to believe and how to live and honour God in the spirit, for the which cause churches were chiefly builded and for quietness to pray: and if there be no church, then to give of that thou mayest spare, to help that one were builded to be a preaching and a praying house and of worshipping God in the spirit and not of image-service.

And if Paul appeared unto thee, what other thing could he answer also, than that he were a spirit and would refuse all thy image-service? And if thou speak to Paul of his merits, he can none otherwise answer thee than he answered his Corinthians: That he died for no man's sins, and that no man was baptized in his name, to trust in his merits. He would say, I builded all men upon Christ's merits, preaching that all that repented and believed in his name should be saved and taken from under the wrath, vengeance and damnation of the law and be put under mercy and grace. And by this faith was I saved from damnation and put under mercy and grace and made one with Christ, to have my part with him and he with me, or rather to make a change, that he should have all my sins and I his mercy and the gifts of his grace and become glorious with the ornaments of his riches. And of my Saviour Christ I received this law, that I should love my brethren, all God's elect as tenderly as he loved them. And I consented unto this law for it seemed right, and became a scholar to learn it. And as I profited in the knowledge, faith and love of Christ, so I grew in the love of my brethren and suffered all things for their sakes and at the last waxed so perfect that I wished myself damned (if it might have been) to save my brethren. And all my brethren that received Christ, received the same commandment and grew therein. And they that were perfect loved me and all their other brethren, no less than I loved them. And look with what love I ministered the gifts of grace which I received of Christ for the edifying of his congregation, upon my brethren with the same love did they minister their gifts again on me which they had and I lacked, and so love made all common. And moreover, if they call my works my merits, I bestowed all my works upon my brethren to teach them, and reaped the fruit thereof, even my brethren's edifying and soul's health, yea, and reap daily in that I left my doctrine and ensample of living behind me, by which many are converted unto Christ daily. If thou desire therefore to enjoy part of my merit, go and read in my gospel, and thou shalt find the fruit of my labour, the knowledge of Christ, the health of the soul and everlasting life.

And as I loved my brethren when I lived, so I love them still, and now more perfectly. Howbeit my love then was painful: for the more I loved, the more I sorrowed, feared and cared for them, to bring them into the knowledge of the truth and to keep them in unity of faith, lest the false prophets should deceive them, or their own infirmities should break peace and unity, or cause them to fall into any sin. But now my love is without pain. For I see the will and providence of God and how the end of all things shall be unto his glory and profit of the elect. And though I see the elect shall sometime fall, yet I see how they shall arise again and how that their fall shall be unto the glory of God and their own profit. And we, that are in heaven love you all alike: neither love we one more and another less. And therefore if ye love us more one than another, that is fleshly, as mine old Corinthians once loved and I rebuked them. Neither can we be moved to come more to help one than another, but we wait when God will send any of us unto the elect that call for help in Christ's name. Wherefore, if thou wilt be holpen of any of us pray in Christ's name: and God shall send one of us, an angel or a saint, to keep the power of the devils from you, but not whom thou wouldest choose, tempting God, but whom it pleaseth God to send.

And if your preachers love you not after the same manner to edify you with the true doctrine of Christ and ensample of living thereafter, and to keep you in unity of faith and charity, they be not of Christ's disciples but antichrists which under the name of Christ seek to reign over you as temporal tyrants. And in like manner, if this be not written in your hearts, that ye ought to love one another as Christ loved you and as ye had ensample of us his apostles, ye go astray in vanities, and are not in the right way.

*

Dearly beloved, let us love one another, for love is of God: and all that love are born of God, and know God. And he that loveth not, knoweth not God: for God is love [iv:7].

John singeth his old song again, and teacheth an infallible and sure token which we may see and feel at our fingers' ends and thereby be out of all doubt, that our faith is unfeigned and that we know God and be born of God and that we hearken unto the doctrine of the apostles purely and godly and not of any curiosity, to seek glory and honour therein unto ourselves and to make a cloak thereof to cover our covetousness and filthy lusts: which token is if we love one another. For the love of a man's neighbour unfeignedly springeth out of the unfeigned knowledge of God in Christ's blood: by which knowledge we be born of God and love God and our neighbours for his sake. And so he that loveth his neighbour unfeignedly is sure of himself, that he knoweth God and is of God unfeignedly: and contrariwise, he that loveth not, knoweth not God, for God in Christ's blood is such a love, that if a man saw it, it were impossible that he should not break out into the love of God again and of his neighbour for his sake.

Herein appeared the love of God unto us-ward, because God sent his only son into the world, that we should live through him. Herein is love, not that we loved God, but that he loved us, and sent his Son a satisfaction for our sins. [iv:9–10]

If a man had once felt within in his conscience the fierce wrath of God toward sinners and the terrible and most cruel damnation that the law threateneth, and then beheld with the eyes of a strong faith the mercy, favour and grace, the taking away of the damnation of the law and restoring again of life, freely offered us in Christ's blood, he should perceive love and so much the more, that it was shewed us when we were sinners and enemies to God, and that without all deservings, without our endeavouring, enforcing and preparing ourselves and without all good motions, qualities and properties of our freewill, but when our hearts were as dead unto all good working as the members of him whose soul is departed. Which thing to prove and to stop the blasphemous mouths of all our adversaries I will, of innumerable texts, rehearse one, in the beginning of the second chapter to the Ephesians, where Paul saith thus: Ye were dead in trespass and sin, in which ye walked according to the course of the world and after the governor that ruleth in the air, the spirit that worketh in the children of unbelief, among which we also had our conversation in time past, in the lusts of our flesh, and fulfilled the lusts of the flesh and of the mind (so that the flesh and mind were agreed both to sin, and the mind consented as well as the flesh) and were by nature the children of wrath as well as other. But God, being rich in mercy, through the great love wherewith he loved us, even when we were dead in sin, hath quickened us with Christ: for by grace are ye saved, and with him hath raised us up and with him has made us sit in heavenly things, through Jesus Christ, for to shew in time to come the exceeding riches of his grace in kindness to us-ward in Jesus Christ. For by grace are ye saved through faith, and that not of yourselves, for it is the gift of God and cometh not of works, lest any man should boast himself. But we are his workmanship, created in Christ Jesu unto good works, unto which God ordained us before, that we should walk in them. The text is plain: we were stone dead, and without life or power to do or consent to good. The whole nature of us was captive under the devil and led at his will. And we were as wicked as the devil now is (except that he now sinneth against the Holy Ghost), and we consented unto sin with soul and body and hated the law of God. But God, of his grace only, quickened us in Christ, and raised us out of that death and made us sit with Christ in heavenly things: that is, he set our hearts at rest and made us sit fast in the life of Christ's doctrine and unmoveable from the love of Christ. And finally we are, in this our second birth, God's workmanship and creation in Christ, so that, as he which is yet unmade hath no life nor power to work, no more had we, till we were made again in Christ. The preaching of mercy in Christ quickened our hearts through faith wrought by the Spirit of Christ which God poured into our hearts ere we wist.

Dearly beloved, if God so loved us, then ought we to love one another [iv:11].

If we felt the love of God in Christ's blood, we could not but love again, not only God and Christ, but also all that are bought with Christ's blood. If we love God for the pleasures that we receive, then love we ourselves. But if we love him to do him pleasure again, that can we no otherwise do, than in loving our neighbours for his sake: them that are good, to continue them in their goodness, and them that are evil, to draw them to good. Love is the instrument wherewith faith maketh us God's sons, and fashioneth us like the image of God, and certifieth us that we so are. And therefore commandeth Christ, Love your enemies, bless them that curse you, pray for them that persecute you, that ye may be the sons of your heavenly Father, which maketh his sun rise over good and bad, and sendeth his rain upon just and unjust: yea, which made the sun of his mercy shine upon us and sent the rain of the blood of his dear and only child upon our souls to quicken us and to make us see love, to love again.

No man hath at any time seen God. If we love one another, God dwelleth in us, and his love is perfect in us [iv:12].

Though we cannot see God, yet if we love one another, we be sure that he abideth in us, and that his love is perfect in us, that is that we love him unfeignedly. For to love God truly and to give him thanks, is only to love our neighbour for his sake: for upon his person thou canst bestow no benefit. And forasmuch as we never saw God, let us make no image of him, nor do him any image-service after our own imagination, but let us go to the scripture, that hath seen him, and there wete what fashion he is of, and what service he will be served with. Blind reason saith God is a carved post and will be served with a candle: but scripture saith God is love, and will be served with love. If thou love thy neighbour, then art thou the image of God thyself, and he dwelleth in the living temple of thine heart. And thy loving of thy neighbour for his sake is his service and worship in the spirit and a candle that burneth before him in thine heart and casteth out the light of good works before the world and draweth all to God and maketh his enemies leave their evil and come and worship him also.

Hereby we know that we abide in him, and he in us. For he hath given us of his spirit [iv:13].

He that hath not Christ's Spirit, the same is none of his. If we have the Spirit of God, then are we sure. But how shall we know whether we have the Spirit? Ask John, and he will say, If we love one another.

And we have seen and do testify, that the Father hath sent his Son, the saviour of the world. Whosoever confesseth that Jesus is the Son of God, in him dwelleth God and he in God. And we have known and believed the love that God hath to us [iv:14–16a].

First, the apostles taught no fables, but that they saw and received of God by the witness of his Spirit. Secondarily, John ascendeth up step higher, from love to faith, and saith, He that believeth that Jesus is God's Son, hath God in him. And I doubt not but the bishop of Rome and his defenders will answer John and say, Then the devil hath God in him, and is also in God: for other faith, than such as the devil hath, felt they never any. But John preventeth [goes before] them, saying, We have known and believed the love that God hath to us: that is, we believe not only with story faith, as men believe old chronicles, but we believe the love and mercy that God shewed us and put our trust and confidence therein (and so taketh scripture belief), we believe that Jesus is the Son of God, became man and was slain for our sins, which is a token of great love. And that love believe we, and trust thereto.

From *The Practice of Prelates*, 1531

By what means the prelates fell from Christ

The office of a bishop was a room, at the beginning, that no man coveted, and that no man durst take upon him, save he only which loved Christ better than his own life. For as Christ saith, that no man might be his disciple, except that he were ready to forsake life and all, even so might that officer be sure that it would cost him his life at one time or another, for bearing record unto the truth. But after that the multitude of the Christen were increased and many great men had received the faith, then both lands and rents, as well as other goods, were given unto the maintenance, as well of the clergy, as of the poor: because they gave then no tithes to the priests, nor yet now do, save in certain countries. For it is too much to give alms, offerings, lands and tithes also. And then the bishops made them substitutes under them to help them, which they called priests and kept the name of bishop unto themselves.

But out of the deacons sprang all the mischief: for through their hands went all things: they ministered unto the clergy, they ministered unto the poor, they were in favour with great and small. And when the bishop's office began to have rest and to be honourable, then the deacons, through favour and gifts, clamb up thereunto, as lightly he that hath the old abbot's treasure succeedeth with us. And by the means of their practice and acquaintance in the world they were more subtle and worldly wise than the old bishops and less learned in God's word, as our prelates are, when they come from stewardships in gentlemen's houses, and from surveying of great men's lands, lords' secrets, kings' councils, ambassadorship, from war and ministering all worldly matters yea, worldly mischief. And yet now they come not thence but receive all and bide there still, yea, they have enacted by plain parliament that they must bide in the court still, or else they may not have plurality of benefices. And then by little and little they enhanced themselves and turned all to themselves, minishing the poor people's part and increasing theirs and joining acquaintance with great men and with their power clamb up, and entitled them to the choosing and confirming of the pope and all bishops, to flatter and purchase favour and defenders, trusting more unto their worldly wisdom than unto the doctrine of Christ, which is the wisdom of God and unto the defence of man than of God. Then, while they that had the plough by the tail looked back, the plough went awry, faith waxed feeble and fainty, love waxed cold, the scripture waxed dark, Christ was no more seen. He was in the mount with Moses, and therefore the bishops would have a god upon the earth whom they might see and thereupon they began to dispute who should be greatest.

*

When the bishops, priests, and deacons were fallen and had received of the pope the kingdom that pertained unto the poor people and had robbed them and parted their patrimony among themselves, then sprang the orders of monks, whose profession was to abstain from flesh all their lives, to wear vile raiment, to eat but once in the day and that but butter, cheese, eggs, fruits, roots, and such things that were not costly and might everywhere be found. And they wrote books and wrought divers things to get their living withal. When the laymen saw that the priests were fallen into such covetousness and that the monks were so holy, they thought, These be meet men to minister our alms unto the poor people: for their profession is so holy that they cannot deceive us as the priests do: and made the monks tutors and ministers unto the poor, and gave great lands and riches into their hands, to deal it unto the poor. When the monks saw such abundance, they fell after the ensample of the priests, and took dispensations of the pope for their rules and strait profession, which now is as wide as their cowls, and divided all among them and robbed the poor once more. And out of the abbeys took he the most part of his bishopricks and cathedral churches and the most part of all the lands he hath, besides that there remain yet so many mighty abbeys and nunneries thereto.

As soon as the monks were fallen, then sprang these begging friars out of hell, the last kind of caterpillars, in a more vile apparel and a more strait religion, that, if aught of relief were left among the laymen for the poor people, these horse-leeches might suck that also: which drone-bees, as soon as they had learned their craft, and had built them goodly and costly nests and their limiters had divided all countries among them to beg in and had prepared livings of a certainty, though with begging, then they also took dispensations of the pope, for to live as largely and as lewdly as the monks.

And yet unto the laymen, whom they have thus falsely robbed and from which they have divided themselves and made them a several kingdom among themselves, they leave the paying of toll, custom and tribute (for unto all the charges of the realms will they not pay one mite) and the finding of all the poor, the finding of scholars for the most part, the finding of these foresaid horse-leeches and caterpillars, the begging friars, the repairing of the high-ways and bridges, the building and reparations of their abbeys and cathedral churches, chapels, colleges, for which they send out their pardons daily by heaps and gather a thousand pounds for every hundred that they bestow truly.

*

And in like manner whosoever defendeth his traditions, decrees and privileges, him he made a saint also for his labour, were his living never so contrary unto the scripture, as Thomas of Canterbury with many other like, whose life was like Thomas cardinal's but not Christ's, neither is Thomas cardinal's life anything save a counterfeiting of St Thomas of Canterbury. Thomas Becket was first seen in merchandise temporal, and then, to learn spiritual merchandise he gat him to Theobald archbishop of Canterbury, which sent him divers times to Rome about business of holy church. And when Theobald had spied his activity, he shore him deacon, lest he should go back, and made him archdeacon of Canterbury and upon that presented him to the king. And the king made him his chancellor in which office he passed the pomp and pride of Thomas cardinal as far as the one's shrine passeth the other's tomb in glory and riches. And after that he was a man of war and captain over five or six thousand men in full harness, as bright as St George, and his spear in his hand, and encountered whosoever came against him and overthrew the jolliest rutter [knight] that was in all the host of France. And out of the field, hot from blood-shedding, was he made bishop of Canterbury and did put off his helmet and put on his mitre, put off his harness, and on with his robes, and laid down his spear and took his cross, ere his hands were cold, and so came with a lusty

courage of a man of war to fight another while against his prince
for the pope, where his prince's causes were with the law of God
and the pope's clean contrary. And the pomp of his consecration
was after his old worldly fashion. Howbeit yet he is made a saint
for his worshipping of the holy seat of St Peter, not that seat of
Peter which is Christ's gospel, but another, lied to be Peter's and
is indeed *cathedra pestilentiæ*, a chair of false doctrine. And because
he could no skill of our Lord's gospel, he said of matins with our
lady. If any man understand the Latin, let him read his life and
compare it unto the scripture, and then he shall see such holiness
as were here too long to be rehearsed. And every abbey and every
cathedral church, did shrine them one god or other and mingled
the lives of the very saints with stark lies, to move men to offer:
which thing they call devotion.

And though in all their doings they oppress the temporalty and
their commonwealth and be grievous unto the rich and painful to
the poor, yet they be so many, and so exercised in wiles and so
subtle and so knit and sworn together, that they compass the
temporalty and make them bear them, whether they will or will
not (as the oak doth the ivy), partly with juggling and beside that
with worldly policy. For every abbot will make him that may do
most in the shire, or with the king, the steward of his lands and
give him a fee yearly, and will lend unto some, and feast other,
that by such means they do what they will. And little master
parson, after the same manner, if he come into an house and the
wife be snout-fair, he will root himself there by one craft or other,
either by using such pastime as the good man doth, or in being
beneficial by one way or other, or he will lend him and so bring
him into his danger [dependence] that he cannot thrust him out
when he would, but must be compelled to bear him, and to let him
be homely, whether he will or no.

From *An Answer unto Sir Thomas More's Dialogue*, 1531

Why he useth *love*, rather than *charity*.

He rebuketh me also that I translate this Greek word *agape* into *love* and not rather into *charity*, so holy and so known a term. Verily, *charity* is no known English, in that sense which *agape* requireth. For when we say, Give your alms in the worship of God and sweet St Charity, and when the father teacheth his son to say, Blessing, father, for St Charity, what mean they? In good faith they wot not. Moreover, when we say, God help you, I have done my charity for this day, do we not take it for alms? and, The man is ever chiding and out of charity and, I beshrew him, saving my charity, there we take it for patience. And when I say, A charitable man, it is taken for merciful. And though mercifulness be a good love, or rather spring of a good love, yet is not every good love mercifulness. As when a woman loveth her husband godly, or a man his wife or his friend that is in none adversity, it is not always mercifulness. Also we say not, This man hath a great charity to God, but a great love. Wherefore I must have used this general term *love* in spite of mine heart oftentimes. And *agape* and *caritas* were words used among the heathen, ere Christ came, and signified therefore more than a *godly love*. And we may say well enough and have heard it spoken, that the Turks be charitable one to another among themselves and some of them unto the Christians too. Besides all this, *agape is* common unto all loves.

And when M. More saith, Every love is not charity, no more is every apostle Christ's apostle, nor every angel God's angel, nor every hope Christian hope, nor every faith or belief Christ's belief, and so by an hundred thousand words: so that if I should always use but a word that were no more general than the word I interpret, I should interpret nothing at all. But the matter itself and the circumstances do declare what love, what hope and what faith is spoken of. And, finally, I say not, charity God, or charity your neighbour, but, love God and love your neighbour, yea, and though we say a man ought to love his neighbour's wife and his daughter, a christian man doth not understand that he is commanded to defile his neighbour's wife or his neighbour's daughter.

*

Faith is ever assailed and fought withal.

Moreover this our faith which we have in Christ is ever fought against, ever assailed and beaten at with desperation: not when we sin only, but also in all temptations of adversity, into which God bringeth us to nurture us and to shew us our own hearts the hypocrisy and false thoughts that there lie hid, our almost no faith at all and as little love even then haply when we thought ourselves most perfect of all. For when temptations come, we cannot stand: when we have sinned, faith is feeble, when wrong is done us we cannot forgive, in sickness, in loss of goods and in all tribulations, we be impatient, when our neighbour needeth our help, that we must depart with him of ours, then love is cold.

And thus we learn and feel that there is no goodness nor yet power to do good but of God only. And in all such temptations our faith perisheth not utterly, neither our love and consent unto the law of God, but they be weak, sick, and wounded and not clean dead: as a good child whom the father and mother have taught nurture and wisdom loveth his father and all his commandments and perceiveth of the goodness shewed him that his father loveth him and that all his father's precepts are unto his wealth and profit and that his father commandeth him nothing for any need that his father hath thereof, but seeketh his profit only and therefore hath a good faith unto all his father's promises, and loveth all his commandments and doth them with good will and with good will goeth to school: and by the way haply he seeth company play and with the sight is taken and ravished of his memory and forgetteth himself and standeth and beholdeth and falleth to play also, forgetting father and mother, all their kindness, all their laws, and his own profit thereto: howbeit the knowledge of his father's kindness, the faith of his promises and the love that he hath again unto his father and the obedient mind are not utterly quenched, but lie hid as all things do when a man sleepeth or lieth in a trance. And as soon as he hath played out all his lusts or been warned in the mean season, he cometh again unto his old profession. Neverthelater many temptations go over his heart and the law as a right hang-man, tormenteth his conscience and goeth nigh to persuade him that his father will cast him away and hang him if he catch him, so that he is like a great while to run away, rather than to return unto his father again. Fear and dread of rebuke and of loss of his father's love and of punishment wrestle with the trust which he hath in his father's goodness and as it were give his faith a fall. But it riseth again as soon as the rage of the first brunt is past and his mind more quiet. And the goodness of his father and his old kindness cometh unto remembrance, either of his own corage, or by the comfort of some other. And he believeth that his father will not cast him away or destroy him and hopeth that he will no more do so. And upon that he getteth him home dismayed but not altogether faithless. The old kindnesses will not let him despair. Howbeit, all the world cannot set his heart at rest until the pain be past and until he have heard the voice of his father that all is forgiven.

*

More: 'Item, that every man and woman is a priest, and may consecrate the body of Christ.'

Tyndale: In bodily service if the officer appointed be away every other person not only may but also is bound to help at need, even so much as his neighbour's dog. How much more then ought men to assist one onother in the health of their souls at all times of need. If the man be away the woman may and is bound to baptize in time of need by the law of love, which office pertaineth unto the priest only. If she be lady over the greatest ordained by God that she may baptize, why should she not have power also over the less to minister the ceremonies which the pope hath added to as his oil, his salt, his spittle, his candle and chrisom-cloth? And why might she not pray all the prayers except that idol the pope be greater than the very God? If women had brought a child to church and, while the priest and other men tarried the child were in jeopardy, might they not baptize him in the font if there were no other water by? And if other water were by, yet if that holp better one mite love requireth to baptize him therein. And then why might not women touch all their other oil? If a woman learned in Christ were driven

78

unto an isle where Christ was never preached might she not there preach and teach to minister the sacraments and make officers? The case is possible, shew then what should let [hinder], that she might not. Love thy neighbour as thyself doth compel. Nay, she may not consecrate. Why? If the pope loved us as well as Christ, he would find no fault therewith though a woman at need ministered that sacrament if it be so necessary as ye make it. In bodily wealth he that would have me one ace less than himself loveth me not as well as himself: how much more ought we to love one another in things pertaining unto the soul.

From *An Exposition upon the V, VI, VII Chapters of Matthew*, 1533

The Prologue

Here hast thou, dear reader, an exposition upon the fifth, sixth and seventh chapters of Matthew wherein Christ our spiritual Isaac diggeth again the wells of Abraham: which wells the scribes and Pharisees those wicked and spiteful Philistines had stopped and filled up with the earth of their false expositions. He openeth the kingdom of heaven which they had shut up that other men should not enter as they themselves had no lust to go in. He restoreth the key of knowledge which they had taken away, and broken the wards with wresting the text contrary to his due and natural course with their false glosses. He plucketh away from the face of Moses the veil which the scribes and Pharisees had spread thereon that no man might perceive the brightness of his countenance. He weedeth out the thorns and bushes of their pharisaical glosses wherewith they had stopped up the narrow way and strait gate that few could find them.

The wells of Abraham are the scripture. And the scripture may well be called the kingdom of heaven which is eternal life and nothing save the knowledge of God the Father and of his Son Jesus Christ. Moses' face is the law in her right understanding, and the law in her right understanding is the key or at the least way the first and principal key to open the door of the scripture. And the law is the very way that bringeth unto the door Christ, as it is written, Gal. iii. The law was our schoolmaster to bring us to Christ, that we might be justified by faith. And the end of the law that is to say the thing or cause why the law was given is Christ, to justify all that believe: that is to say, the law was given to prove us unrighteous and to drive us to Christ, to be made righteous through forgiveness of sin by him. The law was given to make the sin known saith St Paul, and that sin committed under the law might be the more sinful. The law is that thing which Paul in his inward man granted to be good but was yet compelled ofttimes of his members to do those things which that good law condemned for evil.

The law maketh no man to love the law or less to do or commit sin: but gendereth more lust and increaseth sin. For I cannot but hate the law: inasmuch as I find no power to do it and it nevertheless condemneth me because I do it not. The law setteth not at one with God but causeth wrath.

The law was given by Moses, but grace and verity by Jesus Christ. Behold though Moses gave the law yet he gave no man grace to do it or to understand it aright, or wrote it in any man's heart to consent that it was good and to wish after power to fulfil it. But Christ giveth grace to do it and to understand it aright: and writeth it with his holy Spirit in the tables of the hearts of men, and maketh it a true thing there and no hypocrisy.

The law truly understood is those fiery serpents that stung the children of Israel with present death. But Christ is the brasen serpent, on whom whosoever, being stung with conscience of sin looketh with a sure faith, is healed immediately of that stinging and saved from the pains and sorrows of hell.

It is one thing to condemn and pronounce the sentence of death and to sting the conscience with fear of everlasting pain: and it is another thing to justify from sin, that is to say to forgive and remit sin and to heal the conscience and certify a man, not only that he is delivered from eternal death but also that he is made a son of God and heir of everlasting life. The first is the office of the law: the second pertaineth unto Christ only through faith.

Now if thou give the law a false gloss, and say that the law is a thing which a man may do of his own strength even out of the power of his free-will: and that by the deeds of the law thou mayest deserve forgiveness of thy fore sins, then died Christ in vain and is made almost of no stead seeing thou art become thine own saviour. Neither can Christ (where that gloss is admitted) be otherwise taken or esteemed of christian men for all his passion and promises made to us in his blood than he is of the Turks: how that he was a holy prophet and that he prayeth for us as other saints do, save that we Christians think that he is somewhat more in favour than other saints be (though we imagine him so proud, that he will not hear us but through his mild mother and other holy saints, which all we count much more meek and merciful than he, but him most of might) and that he hath also an higher place in heaven, as the Grey friars and Observants set him as it were from the chin upward, above St Francis.

And so when by this false interpretation of the law Christ which is the door, the way and the ground or foundation of all the scripture is lost concerning the chiefest fruit of his passion and no more seen in his own likeness: then is the scripture locked up and henceforth extreme darkness, and a maze wherein if thou walk thou wottest neither where thou art nor canst find any way out. It is a confused chaos and a mingling of all things together without order, every thing contrary to another. It is an hedge or grove of briars, wherein if thou be caught it is impossible to get out but that if thou lose thyself in one place, thou art tangled and caught in another for it.

This wise was the scripture locked up of the scribes and Pharisees, that the Jews could not see Christ when he came, nor yet can. And though Christ with these three chapters did open it again, yet by such glosses (for our unthankfulness' sake that we had no lust to live according) have we Christians lost Christ again and the understanding of the most clear text wherewith Christ expoundeth and restoreth the law again.

The fifth chapter of Matthew

When he saw the people, he went up into a mountain and sat him down, and his disciples came to him: and he opened his mouth, and taught them, saying: Blessed be the poor in spirit for theirs is the kingdom of heaven.

Christ here in his first sermon, beginneth to restore the law of the ten commandments unto her right understanding against the scribes and Pharisees which were hypocrites, false prophets and false preachers and had corrupt the scripture with the leaven of their glosses. And it is not without a great mystery that Christ beginneth his preaching at poverty in spirit, which is neither beggary nor against the possessing of riches but a virtue contrary to the vice of covetousness, the inordinate desire and love of riches and putting trust in riches.

Riches is the gift of God given man to maintain the degrees of this world and therefore not evil, yea, and some must be poor and some rich if we shall have an order in this world. And God our Father divideth riches and poverty among his children, according to his godly pleasure and wisdom. And as riches doth not exclude thee from the blessing, so doth not poverty certify thee: but to put thy trust in the living God maketh thee heir thereof. For if thou trust in the living God then if thou be poor, thou covetest not to be rich, for thou art certified that thy Father shall minister unto thee food and raiment, and be thy defender: and if thou have riches thou knowest that they be but vanity and that as thou broughtest them not into the world, so shalt thou not carry them out, and that as they be thine to day, so may they be another man's to-morrow, and that the favour of God only both gave and also keepeth thee and them, and not thy wisdom or power, and that they, neither aught else, can help at need save the good will of thy heavenly Father only. Happy and blessed then are the poor in spirit, that is to say the rich that have not their confidence nor consolation in the vanity of their riches, and the poor that desire not inordinately to be rich but have their trust in the living God for food and raiment and for all that pertaineth either to the body or the soul, for theirs is the kingdom of heaven.

And contrariwise unhappy and accursed and that with the first and deepest of all curses, are the rich in spirit, that is to say the covetous that being rich trust in their riches, or being poor long for the consolation of riches, and comfort not their souls with the promises of their heavenly Father, confirmed with the blood of their Lord Christ. For unto them it is harder to enter into the kingdom of heaven than for a camel to enter through the eye of a needle. No, they have no part in the kingdom of Christ and God. Therefore is it evident why Christ so diligently warneth all his to beware of covetousness, and why he admitteth none to be his disciples except they first forsake all together. For there was never covetous person true yet either to God or man.

If a covetous man be chosen to preach God's word he is a false prophet immediately. If he be of the lay sort, so joineth he himself unto the false prophets to persecute the truth. Covetousness is not only above all other lusts those thorns that choke the word of God in them that possess it, but it is also a deadly enemy to all that interpret God's word truly. All other vices, though they laugh them to scorn that talk godly, yet they can suffer them to live and to dwell in the country: but covetousness cannot rest, as long as there is one that cleaveth to God's word in all the land.

Take heed to thy preacher therefore and be sure, if he be covetous and gape for promotion, that he is a false prophet, and leaveneth the scripture, for all his crying, fathers, fathers, holy church, and fifteen hundred years, and for all his other holy pretences.

Blessed are they that mourn, for they shall be comforted.

This mourning is also in the spirit and no kin to the sour looking of hypocrites nor to the impatient waywardness of those fleshly, which ever whine and complain that the world is naught because they cannot obtain and enjoy their lusts therein. Neither forbiddeth it always to be merry and to laugh and make good cheer now and then, to forget sorrow, that overmuch heaviness swallow not a man clean up. For the wise man saith, Sorrow hath cost many their lives. And, An heavy spirit drieth up the bones. And Paul commandeth to rejoice ever. And he saith, Rejoice with them that rejoice, and sorrow with them that sorrow, and weep with them that weep: which seem two contraries.

This mourning is that cross without which was never any disciple of Christ or ever shall be. For of whatsoever state or degree thou be in this world, if thou profess the gospel there followeth thee a cross (as warmness accompanieth the sun shining) under which thy spirit shall groan and mourn secretly, not only because the world and thine own flesh carry thee away clean contrary to the purpose of thine heart: but also to see and behold the wretchedness and misfortunes of thy brethren for which (because thou lovest them as well as thyself) thou shalt mourn and sorrow no less than for thyself. Though thou be king or emperor, yet if thou knowest Christ and God through Christ and intendest to walk in the sight of God and to minister thine office truly thou shalt (to keep justice with all) be compelled to do daily that which thou art no less loath to do than if thou shouldest cut off arm, hand, or any other member of thine own body. Yea and if thou wilt follow the right way and neither turn on the right hand nor on the left thou shalt have immediately thine own subjects, thine own servants, thine own lords, thine own counsellors, and thine own prophets thereto, against thee: unto whose froward malice and stubbornness thou shalt be compelled to permit a thousand things against thy conscience, not able to resist them, at which thine heart shall bleed inwardly: and shalt sauce thy sweet sops which the world weeneth thou hast with sorrows enough, and still mourning, studying either alone or else with a few friends secretly night and day, and sighing to God for help to mitigate the furious frowardness of them whom thou art not able to withstand, that all go not after the will of the ungodly. What was David compelled to suffer all the days of his life of his own servants, the sons of Zeruiah, beside the mischances of his own children. And how was our king John forsaken of his own lords, when he would have put a good and godly reformation in his own land. How was Henry the second compassed in like manner of his own prelates whom he had promoted of nought, with the secret conspiracy of some of his own temporal lords with them. I spare to speak of the mourning of the true preachers and the poor common people which have none other help but the secret hand of God and the word of his promise.

But they shall be comforted of all their tribulation, and their sorrow shall be turned into joy and that infinite and everlasting in the life to come. Neither are they without comfort here in this world, for Christ hath promised to send them a Comforter to be with them for ever, the Spirit of truth which the world knoweth not. And they rejoice in hope of the comfort to come. And they overcome through faith.

*

Ye be the salt of the earth: but if the salt be waxen unsavoury, what can be salted therewith? It is henceforth nothing worth, but to be cast out, and to be trodden under foot of men [v:13].

The office of an apostle and true preacher is to salt, not only the corrupt manners and conversation of earthly people, but also the rotten heart within and all that springeth out thereof, their natural reason, their will, their understanding and wisdom, yea, and their faith and belief, and all that they have imagined without God's word concerning righteousness, justifying, satisfaction and serving of God. And the nature of salt is to bite, fret and make smart. And the sick patients of the world are marvellous impatient so that, though with great pain they can suffer their gross sins to be rebuked under a fashion, as in a parable afar off, yet, to have their righteousness, their holiness and serving of God and his saints disallowed, improved and condemned for damnable and devilish, that may they not abide: insomuch that thou must leave thy salting or else be prepared to suffer again: even to be called a railer, seditious, a maker of discord, and a troubler of the common peace, yea a schismatic and an heretic also, and to be lied upon that thou hast done and said that thou never thoughtest, and then to be called *coram nobis* [ie, to be summoned], and to sing a new song and forswear salting or else to be sent after thy fellows that are gone before, and the way thy Master went.

True preaching is a salting that stirreth up persecution, and an office that no man is meet for save he that is seasoned himself before with poverty in spirit, softness, meekness, patience, mercifulness, pureness of heart and hunger of righteousness, and looking for persecution also, and hath all his hope, comfort and solace in the blessing only and in no worldly thing.

Nay, will some say, a man might preach long enough without persecution, yea, and get favour too, if he would not meddle with the pope, bishops, prelates, and holy ghostly people that live in contemplation and solitariness, nor with great men of the world. I answer, true preaching is salting, and all that is corrupt must be salted: and those persons are of all other most corrupt and therefore may not be left untouched.

The pope's pardons must be rebuked, the abuse of the mass, of the sacraments and of all the ceremonies must be rebuked and salted. And selling of merits and of prayers must be salted. The abuse of fasting and of pilgrimage must be salted. All idolatry and false faith must be rebuked. And those friars that teach men to believe in St Francis' coat, how that they shall never come in hell or purgatory if they be buried therein, may not be passed over with silence.

The pain and grief of salting made monks flee to their cloister. Nay (say they) we went thither of pure devotion to pray for the people. Yea but for all that the more ye increase, and the more ye multiply your prayers, the worse the world is. That is not our fault (say they), but theirs, that they dispose not themselves, but continue in sin and so are unapt to receive the influence of our prayers. O hypocrites! if ye were true salt and had good hearts, and loved your neighbours (if dead men be neighbours to them that are alive), and would come out of your dens and take pain to salt and season them, ye should make a great many of them so apt that your prayers might take effect. But now seeing as ye say they be so unsavoury that your prayers be to them unprofitable, though their goods be to you profitable, and yet ye have no compassion to come out and salt them, it is manifest that ye love not them but theirs: and that ye pray not for them but under the colour of praying mock them and rob them.

Finally salt which is the true understanding of the law, of faith and of the intent of all works, hath in you lost her virtue: neither be there any so unsavoury in the world as ye are, nor any that so sore kick against true salting as ye: and therefore are ye to be cast out and trodden under foot and despised of all men, by the righteous judgment of God.

If salt have lost his saltness, it is good for nothing but to be trodden under foot of men. That is, if the preacher, which for his doctrine is called salt, have lost the nature of salt, that is to say, his sharpness in rebuking all unrighteousness, all natural reason, natural wit and understanding, and all trust and confidence in whatsoever it be, save in the blood of Christ: he is condemned of God, and disallowed of all them that cleave to the truth. In what case stand they then that have benefices and preach not? Verily, though they stand at the altar, yet are they excommunicate and cast out of the living church of almighty God.

And what if the doctrine be not true salt? Verily then is it to be trodden under foot: as must all wearish [sour] and unsavoury ceremonies which have lost their significations, and not only teach not, and are become unprofitable and do no more service to man: but also have obtained authority as God in the heart of man, that man serveth them and putteth in them the trust and confidence that he should put in God his maker through Jesus Christ his redeemer. Are the institutions of man better than God's? Yea, are God's ordinances better now than in the old time? The prophets trod under foot and defied the temple of God and the sacrifices of God and all ceremonies that God had ordained, with fastings and prayings and all that the people perverted and committed idolatry with. We have as strait a commandment, to salt and rebuke all ungodliness as had the prophets. Will they then have their ceremonies honourably spoken of? Then let them restore them to the right use and put the salt of the true meaning and significations of them to them again. But as they be now used none that loveth Christ can speak honourably of them. What true christian man can give honour to that that taketh all honour from Christ? Who can give honour to that that slayeth the soul of his brother and robbeth his heart of that trust and confidence which he should give to his Lord that hath bought him with his blood?

Ye are the light of the world. A city that is set on an hill cannot be hid. Neither do men light a candle and put it under a bushel, but on a candlestick and so giveth it light to all that are in the house. Let your light so shine before men, that they may see your good works and praise your Father that is in heaven [v:14–16].

Christ goeth forth and describeth the office of an apostle and true preacher by another likeness: as he called them before the salt of the earth, even so here the light of the world: signifying thereby that all the doctrine, all the wisdom and high knowledge of the world, whether it were philosophy of natural conclusions, of manners and virtue, or of laws of righteousness, whether it were of the holy scripture and of God himself, was yet but a darkness, until the doctrine of his apostles came: that is to say, until the knowledge of Christ came, how that he is the sacrifice for our sins, our satisfaction, our peace, atonement and redemption, our life thereto and resurrection. Whatsoever holiness, wisdom, virtue, perfectness, or righteousness, is in the world among men, howsoever perfect and holy they appear: yet is all damnable darkness except the right knowledge of Christ's blood be there first to justify the heart before all other holiness.

Another conclusion: As a city built on a hill cannot be hid, no more can the light of Christ's gospel. Let the world rage as much as it will, yet it will shine on their sore eyes, whether they be content or no.

Another conclusion: As men light not a candle to whelm it under a bushel, but to put it on a candlestick, to light all that are in the house, even so the light of Christ's gospel may not be hid, nor made a several thing, as though it pertained to some certain holy persons only. Nay it is the light of the whole world and pertaineth to all men, and therefore may not be made several. It is a madness that divers men say, The lay people may not know it: except they can prove that the lay people be not of the world. Moreover it will not be hid, but as the lightning that breaketh out of the clouds shineth over all, even so doth the gospel of Christ. For where it is truly received there it purifieth the heart and maketh the person to consent to the laws of God and to begin a new and godly living, fashioned after God's laws and without all dissimulation: and then it will kindle so great love in him toward his neighbour, that he shall not only have compassion on him in his bodily adversity, but much more pity him over the blindness of his soul, and minister to him Christ's gospel. Wherefore if they say, It is here or there, in St Francis's coat, or Dominick's, and such like and if thou wilt put on that coat, thou shalt find it there it is false. For if it were there thou shouldest see it shine abroad, though thou creepest not into a cell or a monk's cowl, as thou seest the lightning without creeping into the clouds: yea their light would so shine that men should not only see the light of the gospel but also their good works, which would as fast come out as they now run in: insomuch that thou shouldest see them make themselves poor to help other as they now make other poor to make themselves rich.

This light and salt pertained not then to the apostles, and now to our bishops and spiritually, only. No, it pertaineth to the temporal men also. For all kings and all rulers are bound to be salt and light: not only in example of living, but also in teaching of doctrine unto their subjects, as well as they be bound to punish evil doers.

*

Ye have heard how it was said to them of old time, Commit not adultery. But I say to you, that whosoever looketh on a wife, lusting after her, hath committed advoutry [adultery] with her already in his heart [v:27–8].

This commandment, Commit none adultery, had the Pharisees blinded and corrupt with their sophistry and leaven, interpreting the concupiscence of the heart, lewd toys, filthy gestures, unclean words, clipping [embracing], kissing and so forth, not to be imputed for sin, but even the act and deed alone: though Moses say in the text, Thou shalt not covet thy neighbour's wife, &c. But Christ putteth to light and salt, and bringeth the precept to his true understanding and natural taste again, and condemneth the root of sin, the concupiscence and consent of the heart. Before the world I am no murderer, till I have killed with mine hand: but before God I kill if I hate, yea if I love not and of love keep me both from doing hurt and also be ready and prepared to help at need. Even so the consent of the heart with all other means that follow thereof be as well advoutry before God as the deed itself.

Finally, I am an advouterer before God if I so love not my

neighbour, that very love forbid me to covet his wife. Love is the fulfilling of all commandments. And without love it is impossible to abstain from sinning against my neighbour in any precept if occasion be given.

Carnal love will not suffer a mother to rob her child: no, it maketh her rob herself to make it rich. A natural father shall never lust after his son's wife: no, he careth more for her chastity than his son doth himself. Even so would love to my neighbour keep me from sinning against him.

Advoutry is a damnable thing in the sight of God and much mischief followeth thereof. David to save his honour was driven to commit grievous murder also. It is unright in the sight of God and man, that thy child should be at another man's cost and be another man's heir: neither canst thou or the mother have lightly a quiet conscience to God or a merry heart as long as it so is. Moreover what greater shame canst thou do thy neighbour or what greater displeasure? What if it never be known nor come any child thereof? The preciousest gift that a man hath of God in this world is the true heart of his wife to abide by him in wealth and woe and to bear all fortunes with him. Of that hast thou robbed him, for after she hath once coupled herself to thee she shall not lightly love him any more so truly, but haply hate him and procure his death. Moreover thou hast untaught her to fear God and hast made her to sin against God: for to God promised she and not to man only, for the law of matrimony is God's ordinance. For it is written, when Potiphar's wife would have Joseph to lie with her he answered: How could I do this wickedness and sin against God? Yea verily it is impossible to sin against man except thou sin against God first. Finally, read chronicles and stories and see what hath followed of adultery.

What shall we say, that some doctors have disputed and doubted whether single fornication should be sin, when it is condemned both by Christ and Moses too? And Paul testifieth that no fornicator or whorekeeper shall possess the kingdom of God. It is right that all men that hope in God should bring up their fruit in the fear and knowledge of God, and not to leave his seed where he careth not what come thereof.

Wherefore if thy right eye offend thee, pluck it out and cast it from thee: for it is better for thee that one of thy members perish, than that thy whole body should be cast into hell. And even so if thy right hand offend thee, cut it off and cast it from thee. For it is better for thee that one of thy members perish, than that thy whole body should be cast into hell [v:29–30].

This is not meant of the outward members. For then we must cut off nose, ears, hand and foot, yea we must procure to destroy the seeing, hearing, smelling, tasting and feeling and so every man kill himself. But it is a phrase or speech of the Hebrew tongue and will that we cut off occasions, dancing, kissing, riotous eating and drinking and the lust of the heart and filthy imaginations that move a man to concupiscence. Let every man have his wife and think her the fairest and the best-conditioned, and every woman her husband so too. For God hath blessed thy wife and made her without sin to thee, which ought to seem a beautiful fairness. And all that ye suffer together, the one with the other, is blessed also and made the very cross of Christ and pleasant in the sight of God. Why should she then be loathsome to thee because of a little suffering, that thou shouldest lust after another, that should defile thy soul and slay thy conscience and make thee suffer everlastingly?

Fyfield Books

Two millennia of essential classics

The extensive Fyfield*Books* list includes

Djuna Barnes *The Book of Repulsive Women and other poems*
edited by Rebecca Loncraine

Elizabeth Barrett Browning *Selected Poems* edited by Malcolm Hicks

Charles Baudelaire *Complete Poems in French and English*
translated by Walter Martin

The Brontë Sisters *Selected Poems*
edited by Stevie Davies

Lewis Carroll *Selected Poems*
edited by Keith Silver

Thomas Chatterton *Selected Poems*
edited by Grevel Lindop

John Clare *By Himself*
edited by Eric Robinson and David Powell

Samuel Taylor Coleridge *Selected Poetry* edited by William Empson and David Pirie

John Donne *Selected Letters*
edited by P.M. Oliver

Oliver Goldsmith *Selected Writings*
edited by John Lucas

Victor Hugo *Selected Poetry in French and English*
translated by Steven Monte

Wyndham Lewis *Collected Poems and Plays* edited by Alan Munton

Charles Lamb *Selected Writings*
edited by J.E. Morpurgo

Ben Jonson *Epigrams and The Forest*
edited by Richard Dutton

Giacomo Leopardi *The Canti with a selection of his prose*
translated by J.G. Nichols

Andrew Marvell *Selected Poems*
edited by Bill Hutchings

Charlotte Mew *Collected Poems and Selected Prose*
edited by Val Warner

Michelangelo *Sonnets*
translated by Elizabeth Jennings, introduction by Michael Ayrton

William Morris *Selected Poems*
edited by Peter Faulkner

Ovid *Amores*
translated by Tom Bishop

Edgar Allan Poe *Poems and Essays on Poetry*
edited by C.H. Sisson

Restoration Bawdy
edited by John Adlard

Rainer Maria Rilke *Sonnets to Orpheus and Letters to a Young Poet*
translated by Stephen Cohn

Christina Rossetti *Selected Poems*
edited by C.H. Sisson

Sir Walter Scott *Selected Poems*
edited by James Reed

Sir Philip Sidney *Selected Writings*
edited by Richard Dutton

Henry Howard, Earl of Surrey *Selected Poems*
edited by Dennis Keene

Algernon Charles Swinburne *Selected Poems*
edited by L.M. Findlay

Oscar Wilde *Selected Poems*
edited by Malcolm Hicks

Sir Thomas Wyatt *Selected Poems*
edited by Hardiman Scott

For more information, including a full list of Fyfield*Books* and a contents list for each title, and details of how to order the books in the UK, visit the Fyfield website at www.fyfieldbooks.co.uk or email info@fyfieldbooks.co.uk. For information about Fyfield*Books* available in the United States and Canada, visit the Routledge website at www.routledge-ny.com.